# BREAKING
# P O I N T

Fighting to End America's
Teenage Suicide Epidemic!

New strategies to eliminate a
centuries-old tragedy as-well-as
a silent epidemic in our nation

Dorris S. Woods, Ph.D., RN, CS

USA • Canada • UK • Ireland

Note for Librarians: A cataloguing record for this book is available from Library and Archives Canada at www.collectionscanada.ca/amicus/index-e.html
ISBN 1-4120-8565-9

**PUBLISHING**™

*Offices in Canada, USA, Ireland and UK*

**Book sales for North America and international:**
Trafford Publishing, 6E–2333 Government St.,
Victoria, BC V8T 4P4 CANADA
phone 250 383 6864 (toll-free 1 888 232 4444)
fax 250 383 6804; email to orders@trafford.com
**Book sales in Europe:**
Trafford Publishing (UK) Limited, 9 Park End Street, 2nd Floor
Oxford, UK OX1 1HH UNITED KINGDOM
phone 44 (0)1865 722 113 (local rate 0845 230 9601)
facsimile 44 (0)1865 722 868; info.uk@trafford.com
**Order online at:**
trafford.com/06-0321

10 9 8 7 6 5 4 3 2

To the memories of
DR. BRANNON LEON "TIGER" WOODS
My son
who was the light of my life
and whose enthusiasm for living was contagious
and
KURT BRIAN
whose circumstance became a source
of pain he could no longer tolerate

# In Praise and Support of Breaking Point

The topic is most important and very well presented.

—Jacqueline McKeon, CSW

*Breaking Point* provides us with new insights into the tragedy of youth suicide. The author explores the relationship between mental pain and depression as the cause of suicide. Many "trigger" factors are listed which may help to prevent suicide in vulnerable youth. Dr. Woods' model reminds us of how complex this phenomenon can be.

—Cassandra T. Carraway, Ed.D., RN
Former Counselor,
Adolescent Substance Abuse

Our society has needed a book like *Breaking Point* for a long time. Not only does it take away the mystery of why teenagers choose to self-destruct, but also enumerates specific situations that trigger suicide.

*Breaking Point* is an important work for helping to alleviate America's silent teenage suicide epidemic.

—Dorothy Ehrhart-Morrison, Ph.D.
Author, "No Mountain High
Enough"

A very timely and informative work for the lay public. Comprehensive.

—Nelle Becker-Slaton, Ph.D.
Educator, Gifted and
Talented

Suicide prevention in teens must become a public health priority.

—Kay Bensing, MA, RN
Consultant

Working together - individuals, families, communities and government - we can and we must enhance suicide prevention efforts in our nation.

—Virginia Troter Betts, JD, RN
Advisor to Secretary
Health and Human Services

# Breaking Point Warning Signs Of Suicide

(Ages 13-24)

National Suicide Prevention Hotline (800) 784-2433
National "Youth" Crisis Helpline (800) 999-9999;

**Needs immediate intervention**
Experience hopelessness, haplessness, helplessness
Has attempted suicide previously
Talk about suicide
Has experienced suicide of a close friend or relative
Gives away prized possessions
Makes remarks of finality, farewells
Asks questions about death
Has traumatic experience (family disruption/divorce,
death of loved one, change of home residence, recent and
abrupt breakup with a girl/boyfriend)
Demostrates an unusual long grief reaction to a loss
(depression, sadness, withdrawal from friends/relatives,
discouraged, hopelessness)
Has sudden unexplained recovery from depression

**Watch very closely, plan intervention**
Has abrupt personality change

Displays extreme emotional changes (hostile, gets into fights, and/or apathetic, withdraws from family and friends)

Demonstrates occasional episodes of bizarre thinking

Has sleep disturbances (oversleeps, sleeplessness, nightmare)

Has self-destructive behavior (self mutilation, excess use of alcohol, drug, sexual promiscuity)

Experiences changes in school activities (neglects academic work, unruly at school, avoids classmates & school activities, truancy)

Engages unlawful acts, encounters with police (vandalism, stealing, shoplifting)

Gets over-involved with a relationship or withdraws from close friends/relatives

Runs away from home

**May be normal adolescent behavior but watch closely**

Is inactive, appears bored and apathetic

Acts impulsively

Shows rebelliousness

Demonstrates hostile behaviors

Neglects personal appearance

Is careless, has frequent accidents

Has personal habits changes (changes in eating habits, gained or lost weight)

WOODS, WALLOCH, SAUCEDO

# Acknowledgements

A debt of gratitude is owed to everyone who impacted the writing of this book.

Early in the formative stages was Toby's father, who encouraged me to learn all I could about suicide. Shortly thereafter, Dr. Raleigh, Allison's father, provided a small grant for me to attend a conference on suicide at UCLA with Dr. Edwin Shneidman. The conference by Dr. Shneidman and his colleagues was phenomenal, unlike anything I have ever experienced before or since. Even though I had set out to investigate substance abuse and suicidal ideation, the conference provided the impetus to look at suicide in adolescents generally.

Once my dissertation topic was approved, locating a site(s) to do the research on suicidal behavior was very difficult. The prevailing rationale was that any suggestion about the topic may push vulnerable youth over the edge. A psychiatrist at the VA Hospital suggested that I make a request to Los Angeles County Supervisor Ed Edleman. Mr. Edleman was Chair of the Board of Supervisors at that time. He instructed mental health juvenile facilities to be made available to me. My data collection tools had been pre-approved by this time, but I was awed at the power Mr. Edleman had with the stroke of his pen.

After I had completed the dissertation, I knew there was important information that should be shared with the public about suicidal behavior in adolescents. Most importantly it would be an extramural endeavor since the overwhelming majority of suicides occur in homes and the community. My ideas were shared with Dr. Quinton James, also a psychiatrist. Dr. James suggested that vignettes be included in the book to illustrate the points to be made. Dr Edwin Shneidman, a suicidiologist, provided valuable information for me at an American Association of Suicidiology Convention.

Throughout the writing and research process for the book, my friend and colleague, Dr. Esther Walloch, has been a great person, not only for feedback, but a great editor and listener. Our mutual friend, Dr. Charlotte Hostein, has also provided valuable assistance.

I had started writing this book at the time of my husband's sudden death in 1996. My first article on the topic, "Understanding Adolescent Suicide: A desperate response to psychache," was published only a month earlier. He always supported me in my endeavors and would worry like a mother hen when I was concerned about something. However, he never wanted me to go to the copy center or post office in Westwood at night. I am grateful for his support.

Without my word processors: Cecelia Miller and Linda Janssen, I would not have survived this ordeal. My computer skills leave a lot to be desired. Daric Loo, my son of another mother, helped with the front cover of the book. Brian Woods, my own son, put the model on computer.

Manuscript editors Gloria Bailey, Dr. Sharon Bear, Laurie Rosin and E. J. McAdams have diligently organized difficult information. I appreciate their keen observations and suggestions.

Without the help of all these people, colleagues and the

parents, relatives and friends of suicide victims, this book would not have been possible. I do indeed owe all of them a debt of gratitude.

Dorris S. Woods, Ph. D.

# Table of Contents

.

# Preface

Someone once said that "a journey of a thousand miles begins with one step." My incredible journey into the world of youth suicide began with a single incident and has lasted more than sixteen years. This journey culminated in *Breaking-Point*.

As a mental health therapist in a doctoral program, I sought to find a meaningful dissertation topic, one that would keep me engaged and possibly be useful to the human condition. By sheer coincidence, one day the answer came to me. I was informed by a staff person at the Mental Health Center that the parents of one of our patients, "Toby," were requesting a family conference. "Toby," a lanky fifteen-year-old had been admitted to the mental health hospital after a suicidal attempt with a drug overdose. During his admission, I became a trusted friend to the family. "Toby" was discharged, but sadly committed suicide. Thus, the question for my dissertation study was "What effect does substance abuse have on suicidal behavior?" His parents wanted to know "why?" I made a promise to "Toby's" father to learn all I could.

During my formal inquiry into the problem, another parent, Mr. Henry O. Raleigh, whose daughter Allison had committed suicide, provided a grant for me and several other graduate students to learn more about the problem of teenage suicide. Our goal was partially accomplished ii

at a conference with suicide experts. Later, Kurt Brian's mother provided a grant. This book is my attempt to share with the reader what I have learned about adolescent suicide. My journey has taken me far beyond the problem of substance abuse. I found repetitive circumstances, referred to as "triggers," troubling for teens. Most of these triggers can be avoided. Some of the information was gathered from primary sources such as my own experiences as a clinician, observations, interactions, interviews and questionnaires. Additional information has come from colleagues, relatives of victims, the news media, and especially the *Los Angeles Times* Research Department.

Several individuals have suggested that I provide instructive information in the form of practical, field-tested methods to prevent suicide. My response to them and to you, the reader, is that there are no such "field-tested methods" to prevent suicide. The procedure is both unethical and illegal. Besides, the human being is too unique and too complex for reliable laboratory research on suicide.

I believe that much of the problem of suicide can be attributed to adolescent development. Fluctuations in hormones cause internal storms. Environmental complications cause external storms. A teenager may have either one, both or any combination of internal and external storms. As we know, some storms last longer than others, some are more destructive than others. The onset of adolescence may start earlier or later, or last longer for some youth.

I also believe that any teenager may commit suicide if mentally-pained with intolerable internal and/or external circumstances. The concept of mental pain or "psychache" on teenage suicide was my most surprising finding. A psychiatric diagnosis is not necessary for suicide to occur, nor is depression as closely tied to suicide as the lay public is led to believe. Evidence exists to suggest that some suicides may occur as a result of "death wishes."

In addition to the influence of pain on adolescent suicide, my next most surprising finding was the fact of teenagers' inability to tolerate isolation from other teens. Peer interaction and contact is imperative for the mental well-being of the teenager. This was found to be true whether in school, in jail or the community. Teenagers copy other teens.

It is my intent to fully engage the public's help to curtail this enormous problem which is essentially preventable. This effort requires protective measures from families, individuals, schools, communities and the health care system to prevent circumstances that trigger suicide.

Dorris S. Woods, Ph.D.
Los Angeles, 2006

# Introduction

On a wintry evening in a farm home in central Mississippi, chores were done for the day; silence fell, and family members gathered around a glowing oakwood fire. After a while, they began telling jokes and laughing. That was when Ted rushed in from the back porch and frantically shook his mother's arm.

"Mama, Mama!" Ted cried. "Van swallowed arsenic!"

As strange as it seems, his mother did not respond. Instead she started to rock, as if she were in a trance, staring straight into the dancing flames.

Ted's older brother, Herman, cried out, "Where is he?" and grabbed the lantern.

"Out there," Ted said, pointing toward the back door.

The children scrambled to get outside, the older ones in front and the younger ones following. There stood Van, their 15-year-old brother, by the back porch. He was clutching his stomach, his face in agony as he retched and vomited. Everyone stood horrified, unable to comprehend what was happening.

Van's father, "Boss," was not home. He had gone to the adjacent farm owned by his brother. By now, the mother had overcome her initial shock; she stood in the doorway.

"What are you trying to do?" she asked.

"I... I can't... I can't live here anymore," Van cried out from the depths of his misery. "I would rather be dead!"

His brothers and sisters hovered around Van, giving him water and supporting him with their presence. No one thought of taking him to a doctor or hospital.

That was my first experience with suicidal behavior. I was only seven years old back then, but I recall the incident as though it had happened yesterday. Van was my oldest brother and my parents' oldest child. I did not understand much, but I could see that whatever was happening was bad.

Earlier that afternoon, Boss had caught Van smoking behind the barn. He had yelled loudly, "Damn it, boy, haven't I told you about smoking? When are you going to learn to do what I say?"

"I only had one," Van retorted.

"Give me those cigarettes!"

"You smoke. Why can't I?"

"Don't backtalk me, boy. Don't do as I do, do what I say! You didn't do your work yet, either!"

The two next oldest boys, Jay and Herman, were there, too, but they said nothing. Van simmered with rebellious anger, humiliated in front of his younger siblings.

Boss was a big, bald-headed man with an imposing presence and a limp from a benign tumor. He expected complete obedience. He didn't have any tolerance for challenges to his authority. His quick temper kept him in action, putting out fires rather than thinking how to prevent them. Of course, he never knew that we referred to him as "Boss" and ourselves as "hired hands."

The fact that he was away that night was probably no coincidence. Boss would often get away from the house to "cool off" following an encounter at home. He had a keen mind but was easily enraged. When he got home later that night, our mother told him about the suicide attempt.

By the next morning, Van was gone — to stay at my Aunt Mary's house in the nearby town of Hattiesburg. Whether he ran away, or my mother sent him, is still a mystery. We never discussed the incident.

For years, that episode was etched in my memory like a terrible nightmare. Since it had never been talked about I called my mother recently to try to make sense of it.

"Leo (Boss) was too hard on them," she said, speaking of Van and Jay. "They were only boys, 14 and 15 years old. Leo had them working at the sawmill in Magee. Even though they were young, they were still expected to do the work of mature men. While working alongside the men, both got a taste for smoking.

"They were too young to buy cigarettes, so they exchanged food with the older men for them. Naturally, Leo wouldn't hear of such doings. On the one hand, they were expected to perform like the grown men, but on the other they were to remain teenage boys.

"They were always together... at home, at work or around here on the farm," she remembered fondly. "'Come on, let's do this or that' one would say. Van was quick-tempered and impulsive, like Leo. Jay was more thoughtful like me. Jay could stand situations that Van could not. He never got into those big, screaming arguments with Leo."

I came to learn that Van's behavior, so baffling to us all at the time, fit into a sadly typical pattern. Teenage suicide, or attempted suicide, is often an impulsive response to repeated frustration with parents.

Van not only lacked internal control of his naturally impulsive behavior, but he also lacked the skills that would have helped him to calmly assess the fact that a restrictive, painful, or unpleasant parental situation would eventually be over when he grew up and left home. He could only see humiliation and pain — with no end in sight — and felt unable to tolerate them any longer.

Fortunately, Van was able to leave his immediate environment before further trauma could occur. His departure not only defused a tense situation, but also helped to dissipate the anger that he felt over his father's treatment. At his Aunt Mary's house, he found that the new setting and the energy expended to get there helped him.

Several days later, Aunt Mary brought him back to our house. When he returned, we acted as if nothing had ever happened. Later, however, the arguments started again, not only about smoking, but also about playing cards, going to the movies, and visiting friends too late at night.

A parent, or any adult in a guidance role, serves as a model for the child and should be aware of normal teenage reactions to overly harsh demands. Boss would not have been receptive to this advice, but most parents today can be helped to understand that adolescence is about change; it is a time of rebellion and testing of limits. By listening to young people during quiet moments, an adult can lay the groundwork for better communication so important in parent-child relationships.

Adolescence for Van was more like an intermittent thunderstorm, internally and externally. While little could be done about internal stress and hormonal influence, Boss could have been more understanding and sensitive towards a developing youth.

In Chapter One, Demystifying Teenage Suicide, we not only see what causes suicide but also examine the role of depression and look at other triggers that push teenagers to suicide.

Chapter One

# Demystifying Teenage Suicide

*Depression never kills... Suicide is caused by psych-ache. I am convinced that suicide does not occur without psychache. It is the pain that pushes [the adolescent to suicide].*

—Edwin S. Shneidman, Ph.D.
Professor of Thanatology Emeritus
University of California at Los Angeles
School of Medicine

Until recently no one had advanced a valid explanation for self-inflicted violence. At a 1984 conference the well-known psychologist Karl Menniger, who had spent a lifetime studying suicide, stated, "It's a durn mystery [suicide], you know, in spite of all we've written about it." In his award-winning book of 1991, The Enigma of Suicide, George Howe Colt wrote, "No one knows why people kill themselves," and quoted Menninger's words.

Our search for an explanation of the centuries-old tragedy of adolescent suicide has now ended. The baffling shroud of depression need no longer confuse us. Overwhelming evidence indicates that most adolescents who commit suicide do so in the absence of depression or other mental problems.

According to the National Centers for Disease Control and Prevention in Atlanta, only one in five of the adolescents who commit suicide suffers from depression. At an April 2000 worldwide conference on suicide, Alan Berman, executive director of the American Association of Suicidiology, stated: "Depression is insufficient to cause suicide." However, depression can cause mental pain.

Eric Harris, the student who masterminded the Columbine High School massacre and suicide in 1999, had been treated earlier for depression. According to Freudian theory, the rage Eric experienced over social isolation and rejection by his peers had expressed itself in depression. Had he remained depressed, it is highly unlikely that he would have had the mental energy to carry out the incidents. Once he was no longer depressed, however, the rage was still present. His motivation to seek revenge and witness the suffering of his "enemies" surfaced, so he killed others, and he committed suicide out of anger and spite — wanting to punish those he hated. Neither act was directly associated with depression.

Many chronically depressed individuals never consider suicide. Therefore, if we simply shift our focus from depression as the cause of suicide to depression as a warning sign of suicidal behavior, we may be more effective in preventing teenage suicide.

The cause of suicide, however, is known and is well-defined, including the conditions that must be present for suicide to occur. Suicide is caused by unbearable mental pain, or psychache (sike-ake).

The term *Psychache* was coined by the well-known

suicidiologist Edwin Shneidman to refer to the "hurt, anguish, soreness, aching psychological pain in the psyche, the mind. The person may feel shame or guilt or humiliation or loneliness or fear, or gloom or whatever. Suicide occurs when psychache is deemed by that person to be unbearable. Suicide also has to do with different individual thresholds for enduring psychological pain.

In American culture the conditions that must be present for suicide to occur, along with psychache, are a faulty concept of time and a perception of poor circumstances, as when an adolescent has a *problem or crisis*. It is an external complication that produces internal or mental pain.

Suicidal adolescents lack an accurate concept of time. They are frozen in the present. They believe the intolerable pain they are feeling at the moment will continue indefinitely. They have nothing pleasant to look back on, nor anything positive to look forward to. They have tunnel vision and fail to see a future for themselves. When adolescents cannot see the possibility of their circumstances improving and cannot endure the present pain, suicide becomes a feasible means of escape.

Although we can now pinpoint the cause of suicide, we still cannot pinpoint the precise dynamic process that renders some youths vulnerable to suicide when others can cope. Our understanding may become clearer if we do not make generalized assumptions about what problems or situations are mentally painful for a given youth. The pain threshold for each individual is different, and the circumstances or problem situations can vary just as dramatically, as you will see in the contrasting cases of Toby, Amy and Jacklyn.

In 1988, I was an administrative supervisor and worked as a psychiatric-mental health clinical nurse specialist at a

Mental Health Center in Los Angeles, California. There I met Toby, a 15-year-old boy who had been admitted earlier in the week after a suicidal overdose of drugs. His parents had requested a family conference.

Upon entering the conference room, I encountered absolute silence and sensed that Toby and his parents were at odds with each other. His father, mother, and Danny, his 5-year-old brother, sat together. Toby sat alone. He was a handsome kid, tall and lanky, wearing sneakers, denims, and a T-shirt.

After I asked, "How can I help you?" the father began the conversation. It was clear he would do most of the talking.

"Toby's going to be discharged tomorrow. We don't think he's ready to go home. He still wants to kill himself."

Toby's mother watched intensely, her arms folded across her chest. She appeared perplexed. Danny played with his toy cars.

Toby frowned while his father discussed the circumstances leading to his admission. Raising his voice as he addressed Toby, the father said, "This is your last chance to shape up!"

"I don't care! I am tired!" the boy responded.

I looked at Toby. He was profoundly serious — and desperate.

After the conference, Toby's mother and Danny went with Toby back to his room. The father stayed behind to talk with me.

"Toby ran away from home before he came here," his father revealed. "He has isolated himself from the family and has no friends. He didn't like the rules we gave him, such as his midnight curfew and keeping his room neat.

He's been drug-addicted since he was born. This is all he knows."

"We started him in a drug abuse program when he was nine, but that has not helped. He was sexually used at a young age while my wife and I were spaced out on drugs. He has been unable to express his feelings about the sex acts or the molester. He was held back in school for poor academic performance three times. He is now expelled from the local school because of his always being late for class and being unprepared. When Toby was disciplined, he managed to say the right things to get himself expelled; he told the teachers and principal where they could go. He has engaged in prostitution, too, to get money for drugs."

Toby was discharged the following day, as scheduled, with a verbal contract that he would not harm himself and that he would continue drug abuse treatment on an outpatient basis. Three days after his discharge, his mother found him in bed, dead from an overdose of drugs.

Toby's case is a heartbreaker. He had several strikes against him from birth. His running away from home was his attempt to escape from all his problems. He was angry at his parents for not protecting him from sexual abuse and, possibly, for his addiction at birth. He hated school and had no friends.

Unlike my brother Van, Toby was not removed from the stormy home environment he hated. Unlike Van, Toby did not feel relief that his initial suicide attempt was unsuccessful. Significantly, Toby could not find a reason to live. In both boys' cases, the parents obviously had a significant influence on their behavior.

We do not know what physiological effect Toby's addiction at birth had upon his fate as a teenager. We do know, however, that his problems continued to mount at school, and being without friends isolated him. He found that drugs no longer helped him alleviate his mental pain, and saw suicide as the only way to escape.

Research shows that suicidal behavior is a common response to long-term drug use, and physical or sexual abuse. In Toby's case the drug use and sexual abuse formed a double curse, and as a teenager he prostituted himself to buy drugs.

Before Toby left the mental health center, I recommended that the parents enroll Toby in a good long-term drug treatment program. The success rate of such residential programs is good, provided that the underlying problems can be treated and the adolescent is placed in a supportive environment. The parents had wanted Toby to remain in the hospital. It was not my decision to keep him there or discharge him.

Amy's story is one we are not likely to forget, either. It was the day of the senior prom. Pretty 17-year-old Amy and her mother left their suburban home at about nine that morning and headed for a local dress shop.

Amy needed to have the shoulder straps on her dress adjusted. Her mother, a corporate vice president, had taken the day off from work to be with Amy. She wanted everything to be perfect for her daughter's special night.

As the two arrived at the dress shop, Marcy, a classmate of Amy's, was leaving with her dress. After a conversation about how beautiful Marcy's dress was, Marcy said, "See ya tonight, Amy. I think we're gonna have fun!" Amy did not respond.

"It's hard to believe that you're all grown up now," marveled the storeowner as she shortened the straps. "Seems like yesterday that you were the girl in pigtails and bobby socks."

Amy smiled but said nothing. Her mother beamed with pride as she admired her daughter in her peach-colored dress with thin spaghetti straps.

Amy was pretty, with auburn hair and hazel eyes. She was a straight 'A' student and a member of the Student Council who liked playing volleyball and was voted to have the "best personality" in the senior class.

After the two left the dress shop, they headed for the hair stylist to have Amy's hair done and nails manicured.

Antoinette, who regularly styled Amy's hair, inquired, "Who's escorting you tonight, Amy?"

"Bryan Schuster," Amy responded.

"I've heard some other girls mention his name and say that he played quarterback for the football team this year. He must be cute. Is he a nice guy?"

"Well, I think so," Amy's mother piped in. Amy was silent. She was staring out the window as she watched people come and go.

Mother and daughter then lunched at Amy's favorite restaurant. Amy still appeared preoccupied. Her mother noticed but did not comment on Amy's unusually sullen behavior, attributing it to pre-prom nerves.

Shortly after returning home, Amy's mother realized that she needed to run several quick errands. Since Amy's date was to arrive at eight, Amy could relax a few hours before getting dressed, while the mother completed her errands.

Shortly after 6:30, Amy's mother pulled into the driveway. She wondered why lights were off in Amy's upstairs bedroom. After climbing the staircase, she gently knocked on Amy's closed door. No answer.

"Amy?" she said softly. No answer. She knocked a little harder, but still no answer. She opened the door and switched on the light.

"Oh, my God!" she cried and then collapsed on the floor. Amy had hanged herself by tying one end of a sheet around the rafters in the air vent and the other around her neck. On her pillow was a note:

Dear Mom and Dad,
I love you very much, but life has no meaning for me. I am sorry I hurt you.

Amy

Several months after this incident, Amy's mother was still dealing with her own guilt for failing to recognize her daughter's suicidal intent. "Why?" she kept asking herself. "She was such a pretty girl with a lot going for her." Her husband, a physician, could not understand it either.

According to the family's housekeeper, only two things seemed out of the ordinary: Amy had started spending more time in her room, and she had stated that she felt she could not live up to her parents' high expectations.

The clues Amy gave were subtle.

On the day of her death, Amy was sullen and did not communicate freely. Both behaviors were unusual for her. Her parents, who were high achievers and busy in their own careers, missed the clues. Amy saw suicide as the only way to escape the pressure and the pain of failing her parents. She had seemingly suffered in silence.

Amy suffered from the external storm of parental pressure to achieve and an internal storm of not wanting to disappoint them. She did not want to be a high achiever like her parents.

Unlike Amy, sixteen year-old Jacklyn's suicide attempt

was unsuccessful. Today, she is the mother of three beautiful daughters, a public speaker and author.

Jacklyn is multiracial and grew up in the heart of the ghetto with good "street sense." She lived with her mother for the first nine years of her life.

"My parents' marriage was pretty fucked-up. Who knew who was coming and who was going?" she says.

She recalls being on welfare her entire childhood as well as being left alone with her brother Jimmy, who was only a year older than she was, for days.

Jacklyn was group raped at age six. Her brother was helpless and forced to watch the assaults.

"I had met the worst of human nature out of the starting gate. Nothing after that — in all the bad things that follows — would ever hurt as bad," she says of the rape.

"Maybe my childhood was just a litany of violent scenes. And maybe you wonder how anyone could live that way, how could anyone let such things happen. Is it true that people make their own environments? Or do environments, in some way, make their own people?"

Jacklyn's questions are very profound because the environment, whatever that is perceived to be, holds the key to the well being of many teenagers.

"My teenager years? In short, I just wanted someone to notice me. I wanted to feel like someone knew I existed. I wanted a closeness with my parents that I just didn't have. It was always like something was missing."

"When I was sixteen I was dating Joe and got pregnant."

Jacklyn's mother took her to an abortion clinic. When Joe heard about the abortion he dumped her and started sleeping with Jacklyn's best friend.

"I couldn't handle any of it, the loss and betrayal, and

so I tried to kill myself. One Sunday morning when I was supposed to be getting ready for church, I emptied the medicine cabinet...took over 475 pills.... It was my little sister Wanita who found me."

"I was in the child/adolescent treatment center for thirty days because I didn't want to go home."

With the month-long stay in the treatment center, Jacklyn was removed from her negative environment long enough to get over the hurt and a suicidal impulse. Teenage suicide would not be a problem if all attempts had positive outcomes like Jacklyn's.

Amy's parents and Jacklyn's parents were worlds apart in social standing and education. However, neither was emotionally close to their daughter. It seems as though Jacklyn tried to be close to her parents. It is not clear whether Amy did or did not try to be close to hers.

Jacklyn's adolescence was turbulent, like a tornado. The external storm caused internal tension and pain, leading to a suicide attempt.

## Summary

As we have seen, depression is not the cause of suicide. It is merely a masking sign or symptom. Suicide occurs as a result of psychache, an intense and unendurable pain of the mind. The concept provides an explanation for teenagers who commit suicide but who are not depressed, not mentally ill, and not substance abusers. In cases such as Toby's, where substance abuse *was* a problem, the underlying problems of sexual abuse and parental neglect had not been treated.

The following psychic conditions must exist before suicide occurs: the pain of *psychache,* the feeling of being stuck in the present time, and the perception that a bad circumstance is not going to change or get better. Although we know the cause of suicide, we still cannot predict with any certainty who will attempt it, because each individual has a different pain threshold. We must not assume what is or is not painful for adolescents. What we may see as stressful or painful may not be stressful for them. Nevertheless, we need to be aware that infinite varieties of painful situations exist, as experienced by Van, Amy, Toby and Jacklyn.

Finally, parents' attitudes and behaviors can have a devastating impact on the lives of children. Adolescents have their own unique set of problems, as we will see in Chapter Two. The more we learn and understand about this stage of development, the more successful we become in guiding young people toward a more positive outlook and a brighter future.

Chapter Two

# Stormy Adolescence

*If a teenager causes trouble, look at the trouble two ways. One, it's a way of adapting to or solving a problem even though it may not be a good way. And, two, it's a signal for help. Misbehaving teenagers are rebels with a cause.*

—Joseph D. Teicher, MD, Psychiatrist
Child Guidance Clinic, Los Angeles

Adolescence is captured in the eye of a storm. The unavoidable forces of nature during this stage of development make youth vulnerable for untoward behavior. Much of what teens do and how they behave depends on the interaction of both internal and external stresses as shown in Woods' Conceptual Model.

Adolescent adjustment is also influenced by the level of emotional and behavioral well-being experienced before the teenage years. Thus, the well-adjusted child is less likely to experience serious problems as an adolescent. Adolescents' behavior remains unpredictable, however, since a complex interaction of all the factors involved determines the outcome.

14

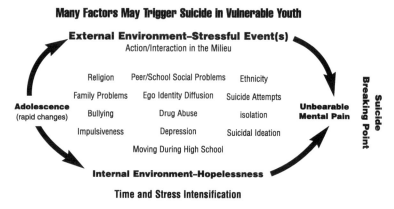

**Many Factors May Trigger Suicide in Vulnerable Youth**

**External Environment–Stressful Event(s)**
Action/Interaction in the Milieu

| | | |
|---|---|---|
| | Religion | Peer/School Social Problems | Ethnicity |
| | Family Problems | Ego Identity Diffusion | Suicide Attempts |
| **Adolescence** (rapid changes) | Bullying | Drug Abuse | isolation |
| | Impulsiveness | Depression | Suicidal Ideation |
| | | Moving During High School | |

**Unbearable Mental Pain**

Suicide Breaking Point

**Internal Environment–Hopelessness**

**Time and Stress Intensification**

Woods' Conceptual Model of Adolescent Suicide, 1996 (Revised 2006)

Probably one of the most useful things someone in a parental role can do for the preadolescent is to plan a period of togetherness without distraction. Adults can use that time to bond with preadolescents and to explain the changes that will occur during adolescence.

I believe that teenagers like those we have already discussed, Van, Toby, Amy and Jacklyn, as well as those to follow, would benefit from "rites of passage" activities at the onset of adolescence. Rites of passage activities would help both parents and teens understand what to expect and possibly how to deal with turmoil on the path towards adulthood. Also worthwhile is promoting activities which encourage family participation.

Engaging teenagers in meaningful activities prevents boredom and enables them to stay out of trouble. All too often "good kids" get caught up with the "wrong crowd" because they are bored. Family arrangements allowing hours and hours of unsupervised free time puts youths at risk for academic school failure, drug use and early sexual activity.

No one knows the precise moment adolescence begins or ends. Variations in onset have been documented. For example, puberty reportedly begins in Europe more than two years later than in America. Individual differences are also found in America. Generally, however, changes related to puberty begin at about 10 years of age, and full emotional development is achieved at about age 24 when full adult status is usually attained. Some form of stress, rebellion or disturbance in identity is to be anticipated in most young people—particularly during the last phase of adolescence.

Early adolescence is the period of rapid physical growth that begins with the onset of puberty and precedes sexual maturity. The age range is generally 10 to 14 years. Young people are self-conscious about their appearances—height, larger muscles in boys, budding breasts in girls. Because the early adolescent seeks peer approval of his or her body, the adolescent's self-concept depends greatly upon how this body looks.

Adolescents might find new sexual feelings difficult to handle. Feelings about sexuality might be anxiety-producing. For girls, other emotional issues might center on training bras, menstruation, and sexual intercourse. Boys tend to have emotional issues around nocturnal emissions, masturbation, and sexual intercourse. For both sexes, uneven hormonal spurts may cause impulsiveness, emotional outbursts, and personality changes.

Fourteen-year-olds are now critical of parents and have the answers to everything. They begin to need to separate their individuality from that of their parents and to protect their concept of self, which is vulnerable during this phase. Dr. Darryl Smith, my professor of education at Claremont Graduate University and the parent of a 14-year-old son, posted the following sign outside her office door: "Teenagers, maybe you should leave home now while you still know everything."

A quote from Mark Twain supports the same idea: "When I was a boy of fourteen, my father was so ignorant I could hardly stand to have the old man around. But when I got to be twenty-one, I was astonished at how much he had learned in seven years."

The adolescent values peers' opinion and may be pressured by a social group to become "one of us." Friendships might be based on competition. The influence of parents remains important, but friends, the media, cultural expectations, and religion might also influence the early adolescent.

Middle adolescence begins after the physiological changes are near completion, generally between and 17 or 18 years of age. During this phase, adolescents continue to show great interest in their bodies. Along with bodily changes come shifts in feelings and thoughts. The adolescent continues to mature mentally as well as physically. A new dimension of social interaction becomes possible between the teenager and his social environment. We saw good examples of this with both Van and Amy. The youth might change from being self-conscious and well-behaved to becoming rebellious. Toby and Van were rebellious as well as self-conscious.

The influence of parents during this phase becomes less direct. Adolescents often withdraw from the family and prefer solitude or the companionship of peers. Teenagers tend to be less trustful of adults and more dependent upon the opinions of other teenagers. They are still working towards developing a clear sense of the separateness or uniqueness of self. Rebellion may be exhibited through experimenting with drugs, sex, body rings, spiked hair, or foul language.

Late adolescence, the final phase of transition from childhood to adulthood, occurs when the youth has attained full adult growth and is at the peak of physical power. The age range is from about 18 to 24 years. During this time, the adolescent becomes less self-conscious about the physical body and less mystified by internal signals; hormonal influence is more balanced now. In addition, friendships now become based on mutual trust rather than competition.

Gradually, dependence is replaced with independence. Adolescence is completed when the individual has achieved self-sufficiency and independence from parents, usually somewhere around the mid-twenties.

Adults who are helping teenagers to navigate these challenging phases should keep in mind how difficult the transition was for them personally. For example, my recall of my own adolescence is probably best described as a rain storm, essentially calm and steady with no major hurdles.

I vividly recall that fateful fall day on the playground at school when the boys laughed at me and pointed to my chest, which was no longer flat. Visible signs of puberty had descended upon me over summer vacation. I could no longer be the "tomboy" that I had always been. I could no longer just put on a T-shirt without hearing snickering. My tree-climbing days ended. My playing of marbles stopped, and I could no longer compete with my brothers in whistling. I could whistle as well as they could, but my mother kept saying, "A whistling girl and a crowing hen always come to some bad end."

So, before age 11, my life had changed forever. It wasn't

what I wanted, and I never imagined that someone else might be having the same experiences. I was as tall then as I am today, as well as terribly awkward and self-conscious because of my height. Nobody bothered to explain what was happening to me, and I was too ashamed to ask.

I was not a problem teenager, but, like many adolescents, I had impulsive moments. When I was about 13, my mother said, "Peaches, go draw some fresh water."

"Let somebody else get it! I did it last time," I snapped. She was as surprised as I that I had spoken to her that way. Without hesitation she whacked me very hard on the fanny. After that, I watched how I spoke to her.

My self-identity had been well established by high school. I had inherited an alert mind from my dad, and I had received positive feedback from my test scores that were always among the highest in the school. When I tutored neighborhood boys in high school math, I felt I was wearing a halo.

Although my parents were not like those in *Leave it to Beaver*, I did have a stable home environment. We were no better or worse off than those around us. The nurturing I received from my teachers also helped me. I think that my adjustment between childhood and adulthood went just fine! After graduating at the top of my class, I felt secure in going on my own. I knew who I was and felt good about myself.

## Identify Development

Adolescence is a period during which youth need to explore the options of personal style, interests and identity. This period is significant for feeling worthwhile to themselves and others, especially other youth.

From this exploration, a young person develops a

sense of self, which is referred to as ego identity. The well-known psychologist Erik Erikson has stated that creating an identity is the major task of adolescence. The youth forms opinions, has attitudes, feelings, beliefs, values, and behaviors which are uniquely his or hers. If the identity a youth has about oneself is one of pride, self-esteem is high. If the identity a youth develops about self is poor, and the youth is confused, then ego identity problems my result. Thus, an internal storm may develop with external consequences.

Kevin, a Granada Hills High School senior, experienced identity diffusion. Although extremely bright, he was not able to answer Erikson's basic question, "Who am I?" Apparently, a blizzard was brewing inside Kevin, a feeling of being mentally overwhelmed and constantly bombarded with social challenges.

Seventeen-year-old Kevin was described by friends as highly intelligent, even "brilliant." He liked music and experimented with dying his hair different colors. He spent many hours on the Internet and had dreams of a career in filmmaking.

Although he was considered extremely perceptive, he was restless. This interfered with satisfying his intellectual curiosity because it did not allow him to become a deep reader. His AP physics teacher described Kevin's philosophy as "I don't care." However, the teacher added, "He presented it in such a way that it looked like a convincing way to live your life."

Several significant events indicated Kevin's turmoil. Kevin procrastinated about completing his application to the University of California. He needed to revise his personal statement about his love of photography but kept putting it off. Then Kevin lost his girlfriend to another young man.

Kevin's friend, Winston, received a call on a Thursday night from a female friend who told him of Kevin's girlfriend problems and said Kevin had made a suicide threat. Winston was used to these comments: Kevin had frequently expressed feeling "lost" but could never explain why. Earlier, Kevin had suggested to Winston that he would go to Washington and immolate himself in the lap of the statue at the Lincoln Memorial, so Winston did not take this latest suicidal talk seriously.

Early Friday morning, Kevin pulled his Toyota MR2 sports car into the school parking lot at 7 a.m., set up a video camera, and turned up the music on KROQ. Then, in a scene described by students as "unreal," Kevin shot off half his face. He was pronounced dead at 8:30 a.m.

Kevin had an identity problem. Identity, or a sense of self, does not form instantly. A child gradually acquires a sense of self through repeated interactions with family, groups, and others in his or her environment. The feedback he or she gets from others helps to form the adolescent's impression of self.

Identity also is formed through internal conversations regarding one's own feelings and ideas. Such internal conversations may include questions such as "Why do people react to me differently when I am brash than when I am polite?" "I wonder why the teacher never calls on me when I raise my hand in class," or "Why don't girls like me?" "I don't feel that I will ever get it all together," is a common lament.

The self-concept is also influenced by peers, by parents through a combination of affection and discipline, by school experiences of success or failure, and by many other kinds of daily experiences, such as work experiences or the challenges of a hostile neighborhood. For most adolescents, all goes reasonably well, and the various influences blend together to form a positive self-concept. If not, the result can be confusion or a negative self-concept, with attempts to alter the self-concept by such means as drug use and even suicide.

## Family Coping Patterns

An adolescent's development and future status as an adult are influenced by heredity and by social institutions including schools, peer culture, and the working world. The cornerstone of stable identity formation for youth is identification with a set of givens: one's gender, one's ethnic culture, one's religious group, the individuals and customs in one's family unit, and the social class in which one is raised.

Of all these factors, the family, and especially the parents, play the most critical role in regard to adolescent development and adaptation. Family stability, freedom from child abuse, and continuity of residence, especially during adolescence, are factors that help tremendously toward reducing the risk of suicide.

Take the case of Randy who, mostly likely, was caught up in a severe sandstorm. He was unable to keep going without his grandmother's support and guidance. Randy was an athletic and bright fourteen year-old who was a member of an upwardly mobile family. His parents had high expectations for him and pressured him to excel in school and extra curricular activities.

Randy was the only black child in an all-white southern California neighborhood. Not only was he faced with the normal rapid changes and challenges that come with adolescence, but additional peer issues as well. He was close to his grandmother who buffered many of his stressful encounters.

Grandmother died. Six months after her death Randy came home from a basketball practice one evening and headed straight for his room. No one saw him take his father's service revolver. When Randy failed to come down for dinner, his mother went to his room to check on him. Randy was on his bed with a bullet through his head. The note read, "I can't take it anymore."

Factors contributing to Randy's suicide include the maturational changes of adolescence, peer pressure and parental pressure instead of support, the loss of his grandmother as a major source of emotional support and lastly, the access to a lethal weapon.

A teenager depends on the parent to remain emotionally calm, steady, and strong. A parent may inspire a teenager by being a role model and maintaining a strong, emotionally secure center during difficult times as well as good ones. Parents need to be consistent, responsible, and balanced, particularly during difficult parent-child encounters.

When parents criticize or discipline, they should be careful to focus on the offending act, not on the teenager. Furthermore, parents need to look for opportunities to express positive feelings about teenagers. Also, parents need to recognize when circumstances are beyond their ability to cope and seek the appropriate help from someone they trust such as a counselor, psychologist or psychiatrist. It may calm the storm the youth is experiencing and turn things around in a positive way.

Chapter Three

# The Family
# And The Village

*As we have seen in earlier chapters, children are not rugged individualists. They depend on the adults they know and on thousands more who make decisions every day that affect their well being. All of us must decide whether our children are raised in a nation that doesn't just espouse family values but values families and children.*

—Hillary Rodham Clinton, *It Takes A Village*

An adolescent's development and entry into adulthood are influenced not only by family structure and function, but also by social institutions. Schools, peer culture, organized religion, the world of work and the neighborhood, all the aspects of the "village," exert influence. Suicides occur in our homes and in our communities, seldom in mental health institutions. The family and its village play significant roles in preventing suicide, while supporting adolescents as they successfully adapt to their environment.

Our children are growing up in difficult times. American culture has failed to help youth understand what is expected of them. Traditional rites of passage from childhood to adulthood no longer exist. Being a teenager in the twenty-first century is difficult. Western society has also failed to prepare parents to deal with the developmental changes of adolescence, creating a rough period for them, too.

## Family Structure and Function

Structure refers to a view of the family as a whole unit within society. According to the well-known family therapist Virginia Satir, family structure is comprised of repeated interactions between family members. Structure shows how, when, and with whom various family members relate.

Family function is expressed by the roles assumed by each member. For example, a husband and father might provide for the family but might not assume a nurturing role in child rearing.

Family members also interact — and have roles to play — with others in the village, such as schools, religious institutions and sports organizations. The great anthropologist Margaret Mead observed, "What the world needs are husbands and wives who live in communities, relate to other people, carry on useful work and willingly give time and attention to their children."

One of the problems society faces is the change in the structure and function of the traditional family unit. Calvin Frederick, a psychologist, writes, "The primary underlying cause of the rising suicide rate among American youth seems to be a breakdown in the nuclear family unit."

This traditional, ideal nuclear family is defined as a

married couple and their children by birth or adoption, all of whom interact cooperatively for the purpose of attaining common goals, but in recent years divorce and remarriage rates have created a tangle of stepchildren and stepparents. Same-sex couples adopt children and more and more single women choose to give birth without the benefit of marriage. The question of how to define a "family" might inspire heated debates for some time to come. Nevertheless, families continue to function as the building blocks of society, and they remain the primary forces that shape the lives of children and teenagers.

In his book *The Enigma of Suicide*, George Howe Colt reports, "Over 50 percent of American couples eventually divorce, and an estimated 70 percent of adolescents who attempt suicide come from divorced families."

Although a causal relationship between divorce and suicide cannot be proved, a correlation does exist. Divorce is stressful for children as well as spouses. Many times youngsters feel responsible for their parents' break-up.

The instability of the family is accompanied by varying degrees of insecurity. This insecurity has a significant impact on interpersonal relationships, as well as the psychological and emotional well-being of every other member in the family. Take the case of Allison:

Allison, adopted at birth, was five when her parents divorced. Allison constantly moved around because her mother was trying to "find" herself, and as a result Allison always felt like an outsider. According to her diary, she hated herself and everybody else.

She went to live with her dad in her late teens. She was not close to her father, emotionally. Although she was very bright, a lack of self-discipline for school work prevented her from pursuing the academic career of her choice. After suffering the loss of a love relationship, she shot herself at age 20 with a small-caliber gun. It was Allison's father who funded the first grant for me to explore the cause(s) of suicide.

Although many factors were involved, perhaps home stability would have prevented Allison's suicide. Being constantly uprooted is also a theme in Kurt Brian's situation:

Kurt Brian had a military father. His mother is a nurse who also provided funding for this inquiry into suicide. The family moved around frequently, making it difficult for Kurt Brian to sustain friendships. Kurt Brian's father was essentially uninvolved with him from all indications. Unable to share his feelings, he became involved in using drugs at the age of fifteen and fell in with the "wrong crowd." His mother sought help for him from military counselors, but he was refused treatment.

When he came of age, Kurt Brian volunteered for the Air Force. His mother was relieved. However, his history of resistance to authority led to an honorable, but forced, discharge due to noncompliance with rules and regulations. He came home, but could not hold a job. He started using drugs again. His family did not allow him to live at home when under the influence of drugs, so he left home, saying he was going to another town to work.

Kurt Brian never left town. He was found six months later in a wooded area, dead of a self-inflicted gunshot wound at the age of 20.

Troubled families tend to experience more "at risk" situations, such as frequent moves, poor or negative communication, sexual, physical or emotional abuse, neglect, separation or divorce.

Drew, an only child, is a prime example of a child affected by divorce. He was sent off to boarding school when he reached junior high. His mother told him, "Your dad and I are not getting along well. We've decided to separate. It is better for you to be at the Treetop School."

The following summer, 13-year-old Drew, a freckled-faced boy with blue eyes, went to spend the summer at his grandparents' home. One morning, he talked of getting the handlebars of his bicycle tightened. Around lunchtime, his father came by to visit.

According to Drew's grandmother, his father told him, "Your mother and I have decided to get a divorce. Things are just not working out for us. I was offered a better position in Seattle. I should be moving there soon."

"But what about me?" Drew asked. His father did not respond.

That afternoon, reportedly upset by his family's problems, Drew found his grandfather's Smith & Wesson handgun and put a bullet through his head. His grandmother discovered him curled up in front of her living room television, a bowl of chocolate ice cream by his side.

As a therapist, I have found that troubled families often communicate defensively. They tend to be judgmental and dogmatic. Some individuals attempt to control others and establish personal superiority, and some family members are indifferent to the needs and feelings of other family members. These variables combine to make it nearly impossible for parents and adolescents to work out their differences, and often foster adolescent delinquents.

This is the point Robert, a 21-year-old, who also participated in study on substance abuse and suicidal ideas, was trying to make:

I come from an emotionally and physically abusive home. To this day, I have problems trusting that people can love me without emotionally hurting me. I am fully convinced that I first started drinking and using [drugs] to escape the negative feelings I had up to the point I took drugs. I firmly believe that drugs and alcohol saved me from killing myself before they [the drugs] turned on me and killed me.

Rollo, a 19-year-old youth who participated in a study that I conducted on suicidal ideas and substance abuse in teenagers, was introduced to drugs by peers. He aptly defined the problem:

I think the main reason teenagers use drugs is because of their parents. If their parents don't communicate with them — and when they do, it is all negative — then the person doesn't have much confidence in himself, so he looks for an escape. He tries drugs to give him the self-confidence he lacks, even if it is false.

## Closed Communication

Parents are often unaware of the impact of their behavior on a child. Teachers have told me about "clueless" parents who are not in touch with their children's feelings or what is going on with them. In her book, *Get a Clue,* Ellen Rosenberg notes, "Our example and our guidance can be significant in making a difference in how they relate to others and how prepared they are to face the issues and experiences that are a part of growing up today."

Closed communication, an important factor in unsuccessful family relationships, occurs when each family member is cautious about what he or she says. Closed communication does not permit honest self-expression or growth, and is not favorable to adolescent development. Examples of closed communication include the following actions:

- Unwillingness to discuss feelings, problems, or perceptions honestly and directly with the teenager or parent: lack of self-disclosure.

Example: Fifteen-year-old Suzy lived with her mother and stepfather. One day Suzy's homeroom teacher referred Suzy to the school counselor because she noticed Suzy's swollen belly. After much prodding, Suzy finally confessed to the counselor that she was pregnant. "I can't talk to my mother," she said. "My step dad said she would never believe me if I told her he was having sex with me." The family was referred to counseling.

- Not allowing a teenager the freedom to give voice to feelings and beliefs (lack of acceptance).

Example: Seventeen-year-old Ida's parents had wanted a boy, but she was born instead. They had high expectations for their "son," and, as a consequence, Ida was not allowed to play with dolls. Instead she had trucks and doctor kits. When she was in high school, her parents insisted she sign up for track and basketball instead of cheer leading.

One day Ida told her mother, "Mom, I'm in love. I want to get married."

Her mother responded, "You can't know what love is. Besides that, you have not finished college yet. I don't want to discuss it further."

This mother might have responded in a more open-ended and less negative way: "Really? Let's talk about it."

- Refusal to participate in problem-solving (lack of availability).

Example: Johnny failed to make the basketball team. He came straight home from school, went into his room, and refused to come downstairs for dinner that evening.

On his way to bed, the father saw Johnny still in his room and asked, "What's wrong with you, boy?"

"I didn't make the basketball team."

"Well, that's your problem," his father replied and then went to bed.

A more concerned father might have put his hand on Johnny's shoulder and said, "John, I know how much you like basketball; I'm sorry you did not make the team. Could we talk about this in the morning?" or "How can I help you?"

- Open Communication

Open communication allows for feedback both ways, to parents and to the teenagers. With open communication, both groups know they are being heard and, ideally, understood. Individual differences are viewed as natural and negotiable and can be resolved by discussion, compromise, taking turns, and even agreeing to disagree.

Open communication in a family allows an adolescent to give expression to thoughts and feelings without losing self-esteem or being made to feel "expendable," like 18-year-old Carlos:

"Parents don't give the attention that adolescents need. We teenagers, we're growing up and we go through all kinds of problems, and we need our parents' support and help, the best of their confidence and trust, and most important of all, their love and to feel loved."

Research of mental health literature indicates that a

lack of parental support and acceptance of normal teenage behavior relates to suicidal ideas. Adolescents need constant attention, encouragement and caring communication. Lack of parental support often carries a message of disinterest to the adolescent, and fosters the development of self-rejecting attitudes.

Unable to cope with the emotional pain of rejection, certain adolescents consider suicide as a way of resolving the problem. This is precisely what Eric did.

Eric was a seventeen-year-old who lived with his parents and older brother. In his father's eyes, Eric could do nothing right. He felt belittled and constantly rejected, while his brother could do no wrong and appeared to be unconditionally accepted. Low self-esteem prevented Eric from making friends easily. His mother was aware of the situation but seemed unable to change things.

One night, after one of Dad's "put-downs" of Eric, the parents went out to dinner with friends. When they returned later that evening, the mother found a note from Eric.

"Mom," the note said, "I am in the garage, Eric." The mother went there and found Eric hanging by the neck, dead.

Eric's mother could have helped by demanding that the father treat the brothers more equally and insisting that he go to counseling. Most probably the father would have declined to attend family counseling sessions, but such a demand would have been worth trying since the father's cooperation could have saved Eric's life. Most of all, the mother needed to communicate to Eric that she did not condone the way his father behaved toward him, even though she herself was intimidated.

Eric's lack of success in resolving family interactions,

as well as his poor peer interactions, contributed to his decision to kill himself. Lack of integration into peer groups, negative family communications, and great family stress can push a troubled youth over the border into suicide.

## What Doesn't Work

As a strategy for coping with inner conflicts, adolescents become self-centered, demanding, and inflexible in their relationship with adults. They become short-tempered because of their frustration at being in transition between leaving childhood and becoming an adult. This frustration makes them less tolerant of adults and more critical, as they recognize that adults are less perfect than they appeared through the eyes of a child.

Qualities that adolescents dislike in adults:

- The stereotyping of adolescents — for example, anyone with long spiked hair, tattoos, or piercings is not trustworthy.

- Hypocrisy — saying one thing and doing another.

- Distrust — for example, assuming that the youth will get into trouble by staying out late.

- Belittling adolescents — making them feel small and insignificant.

In short, conflicts with adults tend to make adolescents feel that they are not respected, not listened to, not understood, regarded as inferior, and treated as incapable of thought and action. Often, it's not the conflict, per se, but the way it is handled.

# What Does Work

In contrast, healthy families communicate in a supportive way. They have genuine exchanges of information, spontaneously help each other solve problems, and show understanding of each other. In these families, parents help children make the difficult adjustment from all kinds of problems, and need their parents' support and help, the best of their confidence and trust, and most important of all, their love and to feel loved.

In open communication, we learn to listen to what teenagers think and care about, as well as how they feel. Encourage and support them in achieving realistic personal goals. Plan family activities and discuss with open minds the things they get excited about, such as rock groups, tattoos or piercing. Talk about the future. Understand that adolescence is about change — change in the body's internal environment as well as the social environment. Know that a child with high self-esteem and good communication skills will be able to negotiate the challenges and changes of adolescence.

Again, open communication is important in both family structure and function, and the demand for it is constantly changing. In open communication, there is no barrier preventing information from being readily accessible or flowing freely.

Some examples of the issues parents and teenagers may discuss during an open dialogue include:

❖ School performance (information).

Example: Alvin's report card arrived home to be signed. The grades were all above average except for one "C" in English. Alvin's dad inquired about the English grade and asked Alvin how he could improve his grade. Alvin told his dad that he did not complete an important book report for the class because his computer shut down. "The book report will improve my grade," Alvin explained.

❖ A compliment (praise).

Example: After Alvin and his dad discussed his school performance, Alvin's dad told him, "You're doing a great job, Alvin. Keep up the good work!" Alvin said, "Thanks, Dad."

❖ A parking ticket (complaint).

Example: "Alvin, I went through the mail already. I see you have a parking violation. How did that happen?" "Dad, that was the day I went to the dentist. It took longer than I thought it would. "Well," his father said, "You need to plan better next time. You'll have to pay the parking ticket."

❖ A question about breaking curfew (inquiry).

Example: Alvin had a ten o'clock curfew on school days. One Thursday night Alvin came home at one in the morning. Alvin's mother met him at the door. "You know you have a ten o'clock curfew. Why are you late?" "Mom, I just lost track of time." "You know what the consequences are. You don't go out at all this weekend."

Apparently, what works is an authoritative parenting style, with good communication and parents who are willing to listen, and even bend a little.

According to Clara Shaw Schuster and Shirley Smith Ashburn in their book, *The Process of Human Development,* most parents adopt one of three general styles of interacting with their kids. Each style has a different combination of three basic factors:

*Acceptance and warmth versus rejection* (acceptance: "I

love you"; rejection: "You will grow up to be no good, just like your dad.")

*Firmness versus leniency* (firmness: "No, Mary. We agreed that you would not go out."; leniency: "Mary, I don't think you should be out too late tonight. You have school tomorrow.")

*Respect for autonomy versus control* (autonomy: "I am so proud of you making your own lunch for school now."; control: "I'll make your lunch for school. I've done it all these years.")

The way parents combine these styles sends very different messages to their children. Over time, these messages are internalized in such character traits as self-esteem, self-control, social competence and responsibility.

Schuster and Ashburn agree that parents who are warm, firm about rules and discipline, and more accepting of their child's individuality produce healthier children than parents who are cold, inconsistent about discipline, and not interested in their children's individual personalities.

Psychologists describe the authoritative style suggested by Schuster and Ashburn as the ideal parenting style. "Authoritative" is a middle ground between "autocratic" and "permissive" parenting. Both extremes have been found to have a detrimental effect on children's competence and integrity.

The need to control children often results in damage to their self-esteem. In his book *Beyond the Classroom,* John Steinberg asserts, "Parents who are high in control tend to value obedience over independence. They are likely to tell their children that young people should not question adults, that their opinions count less because they are children. Expressions of individuality are frowned upon in these families, and are equated with signs of disrespect."

Steinberg also says, "Parents often forget that their children live their lives more according to the way we live than what we say."

Family therapists generally recommend these strategies:

- ❂ "Constructive listening," in which parents encourage teenagers to talk, without the parents letting their personal feelings interfere. To get teens to listen, parents need to talk less. They need to say in a sentence what they would ordinarily say in a paragraph, or in a word what usually requires a sentence. The power of brevity is surprising.

- ❂ Regular family meetings in which the teen can air grievances and parents listen. Whatever the issue, parents need to help resolve it. Build compromise, clarify the agreements and consequences for breaking the agreements, and put them in writing.

## How Adolescents Feel About Adults

Most adolescents yearn for positive relationships with parents and adults. Their ideal adult is one who can listen and understand. Unfortunately, the ideal adult is rare, and the alternative is difficult for the adolescent to accept.

Martin E. Sigleman discusses resilience in his book, *The Optimistic Child.* He allows and encourages age-appropriate problem-solving and to look at different options. Optimism about the future is what we want for every teen. It is good insurance against suicide.

Next, we will see how the village can influence adolescent behavior.

# The Village

"It takes a village to raise a child" according to an old African proverb, still applicable today. Villages are the communities where we reside with our schools, religious institutions, social welfare and health agencies, law enforcement networks, neighbors, friends, family, parks, and recreational facilities.

School, like the family, functions as an integral unit of society especially in the lives of children and adolescents. "A close relationship with the home is an important part of the school" states Lisbeth Schorr in her book *Within Our Reach.* She adds, "Homework is seen not only as providing additional time for learning certain skills, but as a way to keep family and school in touch with each other, and give children the opportunity to demonstrate to their families what they have learned."

According to Debbie Meier, founder of Central Park Elementary School in New York, "Teachers cannot be saviors of kids from their families, no matter how many difficulties the family has. Nothing happens unless the family gets involved. School has to be an ally, not a competitor for the child. [Problems] have to be solved with the family."

I agree with James Comer, noted child psychiatrist and education advocate: "It is essential to address the entire social system of the school because of the way the many variables interact and because attitudes, morale and hope all affect school performance." His chapter on "Suicide and the School" looks at the school climate and at variables that might have an impact on suicidal behavior.

Churches, temples, and other spiritual institutions support child development by reinforcing the moral values of the parents and teaching ethical conduct. Many have wholesome youth clubs and activities as well. The results of my own research conducted at Claremont Graduate University, as well as work by other researchers, show that youths who attend church or temple regularly are less likely to entertain suicidal ideas.

Social welfare agencies are positioned to influence the lives and emotional well-being of children and adolescents. Social workers can provide help for both parents and teachers to solve problems that interfere with learning and self-esteem. The presence of a social worker is likely to create a greater sense of community.

The social worker, trained in family therapy, will help students in conflict management. These students will learn how to negotiate verbally rather than to resort to violence against themselves and others. Most importantly, a social worker should be available on the school premises to students in despair for any reason.

Hospitals especially designed for children and youth are essential to communities. They can monitor emotional and physical problems and provide feedback on sources of stress that may impact suicidal behavior.

Law enforcement's presence and action in a neighborhood are known to influence an adolescent's suicidal behavior. Adolescents fear encounters with the law and sometimes engage in impulsive reactions, as we will see in Chapter Twelve, "Suicide and the Judicial System." Some police officers have not been properly trained in the need to approach juveniles with respect and sensitivity.

Neighbors are crucial elements of a village, especially caring neighbors. They provide support as an extended family might so that the youth knows where to turn in times of need.

Peers, on the other hand, can have a detrimental effect, especially where drug abuse is concerned. The lack of any friends is distressing to the adolescent who desperately wants to be liked and be like his or her peers. Feeling unliked and unwelcome is the cruelest blow. Intervention is critical to help determine why a youth has no friends and discover how the problem might be corrected. Recreational parks and facilities provide space and organized athletic activities. Adolescents fear boredom. A physical activity gets the endorphins going in the brain and improves the outlook. Engaging the youth in sports and recreational activities is a healthy developmental activity.

So the village, with its people and institutions, may exert a significant influence on healthy growth and development.

Chapter Four

# Divorce And Trivorce Of A Family

*Divorce is probably one of the most traumatic events that children can experience, and it usually sets off a series of transitions in children's lives that have the potential to seriously affect their development.*

—Ellissa P. Benedek, M.D.
Catherine Brown

Family relationships are invariably impacted by the incidence of divorce. More than one of every two marriages contracted in America today — some 57 percent of all marriages — will end in divorce. National data compiled by psychologist David Lester reveals a rise in the number of adolescent suicides comparable to the rise in the divorce rate.

Millions of divorces occur annually, and millions of children join the ever-growing membership in divided households. Divorce is a traumatic psychological event for both parent and child.

Divorce not only means the termination of an existing couple's union; it implies the loss of an idealized marriage.

"Trivorce" — the loss of a parental relationship as a result of divorce — is a new term, coined specifically to call attention to the devastating effects of divorce on children.

Critical thinking about the effects of divorce on children falls into two camps. The first group of thinkers holds that the divorce itself does not cause children emotional trauma. Rather, the way the process is handled before, during, and after the final decree might cause problems. The second group argues that divorce has an adverse emotional impact on children regardless of the way the divorce process is handled.

Longitudinal research on children of divorce by Dr. Judith Wallerstein has shown that the emotional impact of divorce on children continues to be present well into adulthood.

Each couple's circumstances are unique. A decision can be made to dissolve the union for any number of reasons. Often too little attention is given to the children's emotional involvement in that decision.

We frequently hear one of the partners say joyfully, "I am getting my divorce!" Many times blame is placed on a particular party, in or outside of the marriage, without thought about how this assignment of blame affects the children.

Since children are not seeking a divorce from their parents, their emotional and psychological well-being are at risk, and adolescents are particularly at risk, as Dr. Judith Wallerstein concluded from her ten-year study, "Children After Divorce: Wounds That Don't Heal." Feeling abandoned, both physically and emotionally, an adolescent who is unable to express feelings about the divorce may be "pushed over the edge" during the parental confrontations that normally occur at this age.

Gary Rosenberg and Sandra Gardner, in *Teenage Suicide,* report that up to 80 percent of suicidal teenagers have experienced the loss of a parent through death or divorce before the age of 14.

Divorce has been identified elsewhere as a significant factor in male teenage suicide. In a paper presented at a 2000 conference on suicide, researchers John Louks and Gerald Otis stated that male suicide was strongly associated with increased divorce rates. They concluded that an inaccessible father probably is unaware of the impact of his absence on his son.

According to David Blankenhorn in *Fatherless America,* "The empirical evidence shows that for every cooperative, co-parenting father in our society, there are at least eight or nine divorced fathers whose links with their children and ex-wives range from minimal to nonexistent." Although Blankenhorn did not make a connection between vanishing fathers and teenage male suicide, he does devote an entire chapter to the deadbeat dad who deserts his children and the cruelly negative effect this has. He acknowledges that, while the lack of income is a problem in deadbeat dad situations, the major problem is the lack of a male figure.

Blankenhorn further states, "A fatherless society is our most urgent social problem. More and more men are failing to support or even acknowledge their children. More and more men are simply vanishing from their children's lives."

This is the crux of trivorce. The trauma of abandonment by vanishing fathers can lead to suicide, particularly in adolescent males.

## The Effects of Trivorce on Suicide

The effects of divorce and trivorce on a teenage male are illustrated in the classic case of Bart. While all children may feel a sense of guilt, abandonment, and hurt when a parent physically vanishes, the effect on male children when the father leaves has a cumulative effect — particularly if the divorce occurs before the age of 14. Bart's case highlights how important it is for divorcing fathers to reassure and remain attentive to their children.

From the time he was six years old, Bart and his father had been inseparable. When Bart's father was at home, Bart was constantly at his side, helping him with chores or begging to play ball. His father was very accessible in those days, but everything changed when Bart's parents separated just after his 13th birthday.

Bart thought that he had done something to cause the breakup, and no amount of reassurance from his mother would dissuade him. It didn't help when his father began to pull away, offering excuses when it came time to see Bart play ball or help him with his paper route or homework.

The change was subtle, but by the time Bart was 15, he could tell that things were just not the same. He felt rejection and pain. His grades slipped. He quit the baseball team and his paper route in a veiled effort to solicit attention from his father.

His mother was so broken up by the divorce that her efforts to help her son were largely ineffective. Bart waited for his father to leave on a business trip before he broke into his apartment and killed himself with his father's shotgun.

Bart's note communicated his anger and despondency: "Why did you ruin everything for me and Mom? I hate it this way. I hate you."

Parents are often caught up in their own pain and anger when a marital dissolution occurs. Bart's feelings of responsibility for the divorce and of abandonment by his father seemed justified when his father began avoiding him. If the parents had sought professional help for themselves and their child, Bart's feelings of abandonment and despair might have been identified and dealt with appropriately.[1]

Richard Gardner, a psychiatrist who treats children of divorce, writes in *The Parents' Book About Divorce:*

> "The broken home in which children have been exposed to significant strife and deprivation appears to be a most significant contributing factor to the theory of and suicide when the child grows older."

Scott's story is one example of Gardner's theory. Below are excerpts from a letter by the mother of Scott, a 23-year-old suicide victim. Scott's biological father had vanished and trivorced him at an early age. Two stepfathers had also left.

> I was married at age nineteen. Although we waited for three years before having a child, we were still at that time very young. I was married for five years, and I came home one day and my husband had moved out. I had never been on my own and I really didn't know if I could survive, especially with a two-year-old child. I managed after the initial shock wore off. My son Scott and I became very close and we depended on each other. A few years later I remarried. The second marriage ended after

---

1 From Adolescent Suicide: A School-Based Approach to Assessment and Intervention (p.40) by W. G. Kirk, 1993, Champaign, IL: Research Press. Copyright 1993 by the author. Reprinted by permission.

a couple of years, but Scott and I stayed bonded. He was a very special son. He could be with grown-ups or with children and he blended well with everyone. Scott never smoked and never got involved with drugs. He played football in high school and was a star quarterback/receiver. He also was on the wrestling team. I was very proud of him. I don't want to say that he was perfect - no one is - but if I could choose a son, I wouldn't have changed a thing.

I remarried, and my third marriage was over within ten years. At that time, Scott and I spent a lot of time together. He was at the beginning of his adult life. We took a trip to England, just Scott and I, as our last big thing together before he started his own life.

I received a call at work one day from someone I didn't even know. She said she was calling for my ex-husband because he didn't care to call himself. She said that Scott had killed himself a few hours earlier. I fell apart. The only thing I remember is saying No! No! No! and I kept asking where he was, but no one could tell me. Everyone was trying to find out more information for me. After a few hours we found out that, earlier that morning, Scott and his wife argued, and he thought that his marriage was over. He was so devastated that he took a hand-gun and shot himself. He could not bear the hurt of another loss.

Scott's Mom

Pamela Cantor, professor of psychology at the University of Boston, says, "The best thing you can do is give children two parents who love them."

Ideally, this can be true whether the parents are married, separated, or divorced, but in reality, divorce can prevent closeness between parent and child. The bitterness of the divorce may not be resolved, and the child may be caught in the middle.

Harvard University psychiatrist Alvin Poussaint shared the following story of Shaka in *Lay My Burden Down*.

Shaka, a 16-year-old youth, was a typical middle-class child in an affluent Denver suburb. He engaged in sports and liked video games, computers, and rap music. He was a handsome young man, more than six feet tall.

Shaka's parents divorced during his early teens. His mother was diagnosed with breast cancer after the divorce, his father now had diabetes, and Shaka had difficulty adjusting to the death of a grandmother with whom he was very close. His father's new live-in girlfriend was an additional adjustment.

Shaka's father, Les, was also a towering man, six feet, five inches tall. Les was an executive with IBM in Colorado. His divorce from his wife a few years earlier had been tough on Shaka. Les failed to recognize the depth of Shaka's unhappiness.

One evening Les pulled his sparkling black Porsche into the garage, looking forward to greeting Shaka, unless he was at football practice or some other activity related to school. Typically, Shaka came to greet his dad with a bear hug. This evening he did not.

Les called out to Shaka, but there was no response. Les climbed the stairs of his split-level home to Shaka's room and pushed his door open.

Instead of finding Shaka listening to hip hop music or engaged at the computer, two activities he enjoyed, Les found Shaka on his bedroom floor. A huge red stain encircled his head. A black revolver lay near Shaka's legs. Les realized that his son would never again greet him with, "Hi, Pops. How's it going?"

Over the next month, Les rehashed everything that had happened with Shaka and everything he had said to him. Again and again, Les recalled one particular incident that had occurred in recent days. He recalled a television documentary on suicide. Les stated at the time, "Man, those folks are crazy!" Shaka was silent, staring at the television screen.

A few weeks earlier, Les had told Shaka about his mother's recurrence of breast cancer. Her condition was terminal. Shaka tensed, but said nothing. No discussion ensued. Les had shut down any mention of his ex-wife, Shaka's mother, and their divorce. "Anything he had to say about his mom, I didn't want to hear," Les says. "Looking back, now I know that is what he was angry about." Shaka's mother passed on several months after his suicide.

Trivorce had occurred for Shaka by his father's behavior towards his mother. Les had not considered his son's feelings towards his mother, nor let him express his own.

Ashburn and Schuster found that children of divorce often worry in silence. They also found that the negative effects of divorce are less harsh when children are allowed to maintain positive relationships with both parents. Although Shaka's mother was the non-custodial parent, she obviously held a vital place in his heart and in his life, just as Shaka maintained a warm relationship with his father.

What happens after a divorce is important. The problems are still the parents' and children's, and not just a private matter between the ex-partners.

In *The Loss of a Same-sex Parent and Adolescent Suicide*, the literature and statistics indicate that adolescent males have a high incidence of suicide following divorce and the disappearance of the mother. Additionally, I am aware of two teenage girls who took their own lives in the absence of a mother in the home.

Psychologist Bennie Reams, a colleague, related the story of Nina, whose parents divorced when she was 13.

The mother left the family home. Nina and her father lived with her paternal grandmother. Shortly after the mother left, the father started having sexual relations with Nina. This continued over several years. The grandmother was aware of the situation but said nothing about it. At some point Nina indicated to her school counselors that all was not well with her at home, but her words were not reported to authorities.

One summer just after Nina's 17th birthday, the father started coming home for lunch and demanding sexual intercourse with Nina. This went on for several weeks. One day the father came home, went to her room, and let himself in. Nina was in her bed with a bullet through her temple. On her bedside table was a note that read: "Not today!"

The other incident was reported by a nursing student. The victim, Rosanna, was the friend of the student's friend.

After her parents divorced, Rosanna came to America with her father for better economic opportunities. She was an excellent student and was to graduate as valedictorian of her high school class.

One day she told a friend that she could no longer tolerate her father's sexual advances, and she said goodbye to the friend. Rosanna was found dead the next morning. She had hanged herself in the garage.

Ashburn and Schuster found that children tend to do better with same-sex custodial parents. Studies show that children with same-sex custodial parents are more sociable, mature, and independent. In both Nina's and Rosanna's cases, they would have been safe had they lived with their mothers.

## The concept of a Better Divorce

In a letter to Ann Landers, an irate child guidance counselor in British Columbia stated that she had seen the effects of parents who [do not recognize divorce as] a serious breakdown that disrupts the lives of others as well as their own . .

> ...while they claim to be so much in touch with their feelings, they are oblivious to the feelings of their children.... All I ask is that parents be a little more sensitive to their children's needs. Even if you are deliriously happy with the situation, don't assume your children are.

To anticipate and respond to the needs of children, we need the concept of a "better divorce." The better divorce is defined by Blankenhorn as "an almost universally endorsed idea for making a very bad situation slightly less bad."

The better divorce is based on the notion that improving the process of divorce will improve its meaning and outcome. "A better divorce means that mothers and fathers are ending their marital partnership without ending their parental alliance," says Blankenhorn.

*Families Apart* provides rules developed by Melinda Blau that include the main components for a better divorce. Blau believes that co-parenting is important, and she espouses the notion that parted families are different from married-couple families, but not necessarily worse. Creating parted families requires that fathers, especially, must be willing to put forth the effort to change. They need to learn non-traditional masculine roles, although many of their responsibilities continue along traditional lines.

A colleague suggested the comedy *Mrs. Doubtfire* as an example of a better divorce. The movie is about a divorcing couple, Daniel (Robin Williams) and Miranda (Sally Field). Custody of the children is denied to Daniel, and his visitation rights are restricted. Daniel, however, loves and cherishes his children. He wants to be near them, so he poses as a woman and applies for a position as childcare worker for them.

His cover is blown eventually, but Miranda realizes that Daniel is a good father and allows him to stay in the family's life. Miranda is happy about the situation, and so are Daniel and the children.

Blankenhorn states that the mission of this movie is to affirm the possibility of a better divorce. He lists the main ideas incorporated in the movie as those espoused in better divorce literature:

1.  Daniel Hillard, the divorced father, is portrayed a man who dearly loves and deserves his children.

2.  The divorced father must transcend masculinity. He changes his appearance and his roles.

3.  Divorce can be good and necessary. When couples don't get along, divorce is best.

4. The main problem is not the divorce, but how we handle the divorce. The judicial system can polarize the parted family. The parents' common sense should prevail.

5. A divorced father can be a good father. Daniel Hillard sacrifices holding a regular job to be near his children.

The movie ends with Daniel Hillard portrayed as a sensitive, caring, and wonderful father, who has remained involved with his children, despite his separation from Miranda.

According to Blankenhorn, a trend is growing in America towards a divorce culture and away from a marriage culture.

> The "uncomfortable truth," says Blankenhorn, "is that regardless of whether or not we change our divorce laws and customs, there is very little reason to believe that the swelling ranks of divorced fathers in our society can be good enough fathers to their children... Divorce is the problem. Pretending that a better divorce is the solution amounts to little more than a way of losing our conscience as we lower our standards... What children need is a father."

I would add that they need a mother, also.

Not everyone agrees with Blankenhorn. Many family counselors believe that some children may be better off in a single-parent home than in the home of a bad marriage. However, a bad marriage and a traumatic divorce are not moral grounds for trivorce. Children remain the responsibility of the parents who produce them. Nothing short of death is more traumatic to a child than a parent's abandonment after divorce when the parent-child relationship has been good before the divorce.

## Proposals for a Father for Every Child

Blankenhorn indicates that the prevailing sense of a divorce culture in America will continue to cause a decline in a child's well-being. He suggests a shift towards a marriage culture with the following 12 proposals:

One, every man in the United States should take the following pledge:

Many people today believe that fathers are unnecessary. I believe the opposite. I pledge to live my life according to the principle that every child deserves a father; that marriage is the pathway to effective fatherhood; that part of being a good man means being a good father; and that America needs more good men.

Two, the president of the United States, acting through the White House Domestic Policy Council, should issue a brief annual report to the nation on the state of fatherhood.

Three, a few good men should start creating Fathers' Clubs in their local communities.

Four, the United States Congress could provide valuable assistance to community organizers, clergy, and other local leaders who are serious about creating higher standards of male responsibility.

Five, married fathers should be asked to transform public housing in the United States. Residential communities have the highest incidence of a lack of responsible male authority.

Six, a few good community organizers need to help empower families and strengthen community life.

Seven, an interfaith council of religious leaders should speak up and act on behalf of marriage.

Eight, the U.S. Congress should pass, and the president support, policy resolutions that strengthen marriage.

Nine, local and county officials across the nation should draft a "vision statement" to identify local priorities and to plan for the future of better fatherhood.

Ten, state legislatures across the nation should support fatherhood by regulating sperm banks.

Eleven, a few well-known professional athletes should organize a public service campaign on the importance of fatherhood.

Twelve, a few prominent family scholars could write new textbooks for high school students about marriage and parenthood.

Whether these proposals will work is not known, but they would increase conscious awareness about the magnitude of the problem.

## Suggestions for Custodial Co-parents

Before separation and divorce occurs, children are usually aware that their parents are having problems.

"Caught in the Middle" is a television program featuring children of divorce who are encouraged to express their feelings. The children on the program state over and over that parents need to discuss their problems with them. "We are not stupid! We knew something was wrong!"

In "Mr. Rogers Talks With Parents", Fred Rogers suggests telling the children that parents are having grown-up problems, using words like, "We don't seem to be able to agree on things anymore." However, telling the children ahead of a separation will not always be possible. The parents might not have discussed telling the children before a crisis arises, or one spouse leaves suddenly.

Some other suggestions for helping a child with divorce are made by Loriann Hoff Oberlin in *Surviving Separation and Divorce*:

Reassure your children that your break-up had nothing do with them.

Reassure your children that both parents love them.

Maintain consistency and discipline. Relaxing the rules will not provide stability.

Allow children to experience their own emotions and help them to cope with difficult feelings.

Remember to be the parent.

Do not overindulge them or overcompensate.

\* \* \*

Additional helpful suggestions are provided by Dr. Elissa Benedek in *How to Help Your Child Overcome Divorce:*

Help your children understand what separation and divorce mean in your special situation.

Tell your children how the divorce will affect them in language appropriate to their age-level.

Reassure your children that they will continue to be loved and cared for.

Keep your relationship with your ex-spouse as conflict-free as possible; protect your children from any conflict between the two of you.

Cooperate with your ex-spouse in matters pertaining to your children.

Help your children to feel good about themselves as unique and valued individuals.

Chapter Five

# The School

*"We know that when an adolescent is in trouble, the first person they turn to is not a parent, not a school counselor, not a clergy person, not a mental health professional. The first person they turn to is a peer."*

—Terry Lipton, M.D. Psychiatrist
Co-Founder, Teen Line
Cedars-Sinai Medical Center
Los Angeles

Our nation is in the grips of a suicide epidemic, according to a 1999 Surgeon General's Report, "A Call To Action to Prevent Suicide." Schools share a central responsibility in preventing these tragedies as well as other forms of violence.

Marlene Wong, Director of Mental Health, Crisis Intervention Teams, Suicide Prevention for the Los Angeles Unified School District, explains:

You can't separate a school from the community surrounding it. In Los Angeles and elsewhere, children are at risk for a variety of reasons . . Mom and Dad [are] preoccupied with survival issues that don't leave time for developing crucial warm relations with their children. Many children have no one at school they can relate to, even a class they are doing well in. Or they have poor social skills and can't make or keep friends. So who do these children hang with? People and peers who may be a negative influence and are themselves at risk for school failure [and suicide].

Schools have, or should have, a close working relationship with both teenagers and their parents. Even much of the teenager's out-of-class time is concentrated around school — preparing for school, being at school, getting to and from school, or participating in extracurricular activities. More work needs to be done:

- Despite the close relationship schools should have with teens and parents, school officials are reluctant to educate teachers and administrators in suicide prevention, or to develop a school-based suicide prevention program.

- Some school administrators and teachers are not aware of the impact their own words and behavior can have on a student, or how the school environment can push the student towards suicide.

- Students are the first line of defense against suicide. Many schools have failed to both recognize and utilize the students themselves in identifying and reporting other students who have coping problems or are entertaining ideas of suicide.

- An effective school-based suicide prevention program, such as a peer counseling program, should be developed.

## Problems Developing School-Based Suicide Prevention Programs

According to Michael Peck, co-director of the California Suicide Prevention Program and a well-known authority on adolescent suicide prevention,

Schools and school administrators are defensive about initiating suicide prevention programs in their schools. There is fear that if a suicide occurs, the community will point to the school. Many schools are confused, panicked and uncertain about how to deal with the problem.

Charlotte Ross, Director of the Youth Suicide National Center in San Mateo, California, explained the problem this way: "Schools are not in business to prevent suicide."

While suicide rarely occurs at school, some students give warning signs to other students that they are leaving school to commit suicide. Such was the case with Bonnie, a 16-year-old, as reported by the Director of Cedars Sinai Medical Center, Teen Suicide Prevention Hotline.

Bonnie was sitting in class, thinking about her failing grades and how meaningless her life had become. She decided she would leave class spontaneously and carry out her plan to kill herself. Before she left, she wrote a note to her friend, Daisy.

Bonnie passed the note to Daisy, but Mike, another classmate, intercepted it, read the contents and followed Bonnie out of the classroom. He prevented the suicide by talking and listening to her. Bonnie was able to share feelings with Mike that she could never share with her father. She told Mike:

> I have not been happy since my mom walked out on us three years ago. I was expected to I do the housework and cook the family meals. My dad does not allow me to date or have friends stay overnight. He just doesn't understand how I feel. I am failing in school, but I can't concentrate on studying anymore.

Along with an array of adult resources, Mike spent the next three months supporting Bonnie through her primary problems. This incident makes a strong case for involving students in the school suicide prevention process.

Without educating the students and giving them, permission to tell a responsible adult about the information may otherwise be held in confidence, as students may believe they are "snitching" on a friend, and the friendship will be lost. Or they may not take the other student seriously.

Although community effort is needed for a suicide prevention program to be effective, states should mandate that every middle and high school have a suicide prevention program in place. *Parents should demand that this happen.* Suicide is an equal-opportunity event. Both wealthy and poor kids kill themselves. The program should also include parents.

Future teacher education programs need to have gatekeeper training for teachers and administrators, who will learn to identify suicide warning signs in others and refer at-risk youth to appropriate mental health services.

# Problems in the School Environment

## Teachers and Administrators

Sometimes thoughtless comments by teachers and administrators further influence suicidal behavior. Take the case of Randy:

Randy was a sensitive 17-year-old, whose home life was made chaotic by an abusive alcoholic stepfather who constantly berated him. One day, Randy and his friend Gil went home at lunchtime to get Randy's English Literature term paper that he had forgotten. His mother made lunch for the two of them. While they were eating, Randy's stepfather came into the kitchen.

"Damn you!" he said. "I see it's not enough for you to eat me out of house and home. You have to bring your friend in to help!"

Embarrassed, Randy almost choked on his sandwich. He hoped that his stepfather would stop talking about his friend.

"You find time to run home, but you never find time to get a job."

"Leave him alone," his mother said.

Quickly getting up from the table, Randy said, "It's okay, Mom. He's never going to change. I can fix it! C'mon, Gil."

The two headed for Randy's room. Randy went straight to the bottom desk drawer and took out a small revolver. "I am so sick of him," he said, pointing the gun to his head.

"No, you can't do that!" Gil shouted, knocking the revolver to the floor. "He's not worth it." Gil picked up the gun and held it away from Randy. "You have your whole life ahead of you."

The two had been sitting on Randy's bed for a short while when Gil said, "Let's get back to school." Gil reported the incident to the English teacher, who referred Randy to the principal.

The principal scolded Randy: "Don't you have anything better to do with your time?"

When Randy arrived at home, he promptly put a bullet through his temple. The incident was reported by Gil.

The principal had made the mistake of taking the problem too lightly. A more effective response would have been, "Tell me, Randy, where do you hurt... and how can I help?" An effective action would have been a referral to a trained professional for follow-up care, perhaps in a community facility.

Similarly, a teacher makes the same kind of mistake with June. June was a pretty, vivacious sophomore:

After cheerleading practice one sunny afternoon, June decided to take a short cut to the school print shop to pick up flyers for a school project. June ducked between buildings in a less-traveled area of the school grounds. As she exited the print shop, lurking in the bushes was a big, tall, unshaven man with a switchblade. He jumped out of the bushes at June.

"Oh, no!" June gasped, putting her hands to her mouth.

The man grabbed her. Holding one hand over her mouth and putting the knife to her throat, he said, "You make another sound and I will slit your throat. You got that?"

June nodded that she did. The man pulled her shorts down, ripping them, pushed her to the ground, and then raped her.

Visibly shaken and upset, she went to her homeroom teacher for help. Waving her hand as if to say "Go on, get out," the teacher said, "Go to the locker room!" Receiving no further directions at that crucial moment, June felt violated, hurt and worthless. Later, she attempted suicide by hanging herself.

The teacher explained later that she meant for June to go to the locker room and wait until help arrived. A more appropriate response would have been, "Sit here while I get someone to go with you to the nurse's office," or "I'll call the police."

## Counseling and Guidance

Counseling and guidance require observing verbal and nonverbal behavior of students and

• Taking appropriate action

*Example:* The counselor observes 13-year-old Matthew's angry expression each time he is sent to the vice-principal for discipline. She arranges a conference with the parents and Matthew before violence erupts.

• Listening to students' problems and issues

*Example:* Joyce is a popular ninth-grader. She likes to attend parties with her friends who drink and do drugs. They pressure her to do likewise. The counselor advises Joyce to continue her resistance and look for new friends who don't use.

• Steering in the right direction

*Example:* Mrs. Harris, the counselor, is aware that Peter's mother is an apathetic parent. Peter's attitude toward school is very lax and he is always late getting to school, often without his homework. She arranges for Peter to come to her office, where she helps structure his time to get his homework done and get to school on time. Once a week he comes to her office for a "progress report." Peter is happy about the attention he's getting from Mrs. Harris.

- Steering toward a chosen and correct path

*Example:* Mrs. Harris, the counselor, also observes that Peter is an only child. He likes basketball and plays well. She recommends a "big brother" for him who plays basketball and lives in town.

High school students need to be encouraged to see a counselor when problems develop. But in a survey conducted by Charlotte Ross, school counselors ranked last in a listing of those in whom teenagers would confide. Counselors should work toward being more visible and approachable.

According to Mitch Anthony, a high school counselor, "statistics show that 75 to 80 percent of successful suicide prevention counseling is done by non-professional counselors." He has provided a list of time-proven tips for lay counselors that are helpful when dealing with a sensitive situation:

- Be calm and affirmative.
- Instill hope and buy time.
- Try to focus on the problem, the proverbial straw that might "break the camel's back."
- Use yourself as an example when it is appropriate, e.g., "When I've been really down, I..."
- Normalize thoughts of suicide, e.g., "It's common

for people to feel so helpless that they think about ending their lives."

- Ask if they have felt this way before and, if so, what they did to feel better.

- Ask, "What are you doing in your life that you don't want to be doing? What are your dreams?" (Explore this area, looking for an opening to instill hope.)

- Give them some feedback about their attributes, talents and virtues that you perceive. This builds a sense of worth.

- Ask if it would be helpful to sign an agreement to not harm him/herself.

- Ask about their support system (family, friends, counselors). "Who do you like to talk to when you're feeling down?"

- Share yourself and your resources. It helps them see that we all need other people.

- Take charge if the situation is serious, and let them know that you are going to aid them in surviving and nothing else.

- Do not say that everything will be all right. Don't use clichés like "pull yourself together."

- Don't tell them about someone who "has it worse."

- Help them undo any plan they may have set for their own self-destruction.

- Help them determine what needs to be changed to avoid circling back to where they are.

- Help identify the resources needed to improve things (people, literature, etc.).

- Arrange for future contact to check on student's progress.

- Encourage the person to get in touch with other helping individuals, such as a counselor or minister.

- Call the police if a situation is immediately life-threatening.

- Call the resource person — i.e., family friend or counselor — in the student's presence so as to demonstrate open relationship.

- Do not leave a high-risk, actively suicidal person alone.

- Know you have done all you can do to handle the crisis.

- Give yourself credit for being willing to take a risk with this teenager.

## Discipline

Discipline is the process and means used by schools to shape and guide children toward desired behavior. Teachers encourage good behavior because it makes life easier for them. We discourage poor or negative behavior because it annoys us. Also, negative behavior can be self-destructive as well as destructive to others and to property.

Some forms of discipline for negative behavior may be perceived as punishment, humiliation, or as "picking on" the child:

Thirteen-year-old John had a behavioral problem and a bad attitude. He was described as a boy "having a real tough time growing up." He had recently returned from living with his father in Arizona to join his mother in California, with the hope that he would benefit from his new school's disciplined structure. But he was not conforming to the school's dress code.

The principal and John had previously established a contract to improve the negative behavior. One day the eighth-grader met with the principal to determine progress.

Obviously annoyed, the principal told John he was "doing okay" with the dress code, but added, "You still need to work on your bad attitude." John left campus and returned to school 90 minutes later. Without warning, he leveled a shotgun and shot the principal in the face. For whatever reasons, John had had as much as he could handle emotionally. The principal's comments pushed him over the edge.

John's body was later found in an outside walkway, the shotgun at his feet.

Since adolescents are notorious for testing the authority of parents, teachers, and other adult leaders, Dr. James Dobson at the University of Southern California and author of *Focus on the Family*, suggests handling discipline problems without using anger. He says the most common mistake adults make is using anger to motivate instead of using action.

In other words, adults should take action to enforce previously identified rules, limits and boundaries. They should not get angry, call the teenager names or belittle them. They should ignore such remarks as "I don't care," and just enforce the discipline. Afterward, they can discuss how to avoid the same problem in the future.

Parents help schools with discipline by enforcing their own rules at home and helping the teenager understand that the rules at school will be enforced if necessary, and that bad behavior has consequences.

## Poor School Achievement

Disappointing grades and poor school performance often cause bad feelings which can lead to failure, truancy, dropping out, run-away behavior, and even suicide. The student is embarrassed or ashamed to go to school. Parents should attempt to identify what the student's problems are at school and help the student. Parents should work in partnership with the school.

A research study conducted by Selma Lewis and funded by the National Institutes of Mental Health showed that adolescents who attempted suicide had significantly lower school achievement than those who did not. The relationship between attempted suicide and low school achievement seems to be explained by the untoward behavior of the suicide attempt.

For example, a student who has been performing well and suddenly receives poorer grades, for any reason, may get depressed as a result. It is a loss for the student and often a lowering of self-esteem. Other negative experiences can often *make things* worse.

Todd had been reprimanded at home. He was under pressure to "improve" his grades. He was afraid of being more harshly disciplined for not doing better at school.

A Los Angeles jogger found 15-year-old Todd hanging from a tree. His suicide note indicated that he could not give his failing report card to his parents.

A reluctance to work in partnership with the school is also apparent in the case of Allan's father:

At North Hollywood High School, 16-year-old Allan

came to school with a short-sleeved shirt, disclosing self-inflicted slash marks up and down his arms.

When the dean of students called Allan's father, the father said, "He's going through something. He has to go through it like everybody else."

The dean should have strongly suggested to the father that the three of them discuss what was going on with Allan. Allan was a low-achieving student at the time, and, eventually, dropped out of school.

Absenteeism, truancy, and a lack of interest in school are precursors to school failure and dropping out. School attendance offices help parents by reporting absences from school as soon as they begin. Teachers help parents by making an early assessment report, with suggestions if necessary.

Beverly Hills High School does an excellent job of keeping track of student academic progress and attendance. The school makes referrals to The Maple Counseling Center for other problems. The school assumes some responsibility for the students' learning. This is not true of all schools, and many students "fall through the cracks."

In the town of Bergenfield, New Jersey, four teenagers engaged in a suicide pact. Three were high school dropouts, and the fourth student had been suspended a month earlier. Bergenfield High School was criticized by parents and students for not doing enough to prevent dropouts, and later the suicides of these students.

"Dropouts don't have a natural support system at school anymore, and frequently not at home either," advised Duane Ryerson, director of Bergenfield County's Adolescent Suicide Awareness Program. Four other teenage dropouts in Bergenfield had committed suicide within the previous year.

Bill Honig, former California Superintendent of Public Instruction, writes, "The more emotionally linked [students are] to the school, the better the classroom performance. Teachers with high expectations that all their students will learn, regularly and frequently review the students' progress. The key to preventing failure in school is helping them."

Teachers can help prevent failure and dropping out by:

- Reminding parents at the beginning of the school year that the student's education is still a partnership between the teacher and the parent.

- Reminding parents that attendance, homework, grades, promotion and graduation can be positively influenced by their attention.

- When possible, using peer tutors to help students improve course work.

- Allowing parents to volunteer at school when possible. The importance of education is emphasized with the parent's presence.

- Having the student teach the parent what he or she learned through the homework assignments. Encourage his or her best effort.

- Recognizing hard work and improvement. Example: "I really am proud of all your efforts. You will be doing much better, too."

Parents can help students be successful by following these suggestions that I used with my own three children:

- Working close partnership with the teachers.

Knowing what the expectations are, especially if the student is having academic problems.

- Keeping close tabs on assignments and homework, seeing that they are completed.
- Not allowing absenteeism and truancy.
- Getting help for difficult subjects like chemistry if you are unable to help. The teacher may be able to recommend a tutor.
- Providing a home atmosphere that encourages learning. For example, discussing the school day at dinner. Try to learn what stresses the student, then plan strategies to relieve it.
- Attending parent conferences.
- Attending school open houses.
- Keeping a positive attitude toward school, learning and education.
- Letting students know you care about them. Students perform better in school when they have less to worry about outside school. Support your students.

Dr. James Comer, a well-known psychiatrist and education activist for children, stated that there are three groups of students in school:

We have kids that learn no matter what happens. They are particularly bright and curious and have a lot of support at home.

A majority of kids in all school systems are in this second group, where there is just enough support at home so that with adequate support in school they would be able to learn.

Then there are a small number who really need extra help beyond that. We are losing a lot of kids who would learn if we had a different kind of system. The school can provide that, or it can get help for that student and family from outside the school."

Dr. Comer likens the school's impact on child development to the family's:

They [schools] do not have their effect through the specific skills they transmit alone, but through their values, climate and quality of relationships. Children learn by internalizing the attitudes, values and ways of meaningful others [people], then, whatever content you expose them to, they learn it.

## Failure Resulting from Athletic Teaming

Athletic teaming refers to the decisions sport coaches must make about which students stay and who will be "cut" from a team in order to meet athletic regulations. Being released from the team may cause an athlete to have sense of failure that "I don't measure up" or "I am no good."

Mitch Anthony, Founder and Director of the National Suicide Education Center in Rochester, Minnesota, provides the following example:

I picked up the phone to hear a very distraught principal say, 'Last night, our star basketball player shot himself. Now there is talk of a possible suicide pact. The atmosphere in this school is very intense, and we are afraid of things getting out of hand. We'd like to hear your opinion on this.

A better way must be found to deal with these kids. Something like this makes me wonder if we should ever subject a young person to a team selection process in which some become stars with the problems stars face, and others run the risk of facing the severe embarrassment and rejection of being cut.

In a similar incident, a small-town football coach, on the day of cuts, had walked into the locker room afterwards to find one of the rejected players dead by hanging.

Similarly, a baffling case at University High School in Los Angeles, California, football Coach Bob Ratcliffe experienced difficulty in coming to terms with the act of Russell, one of his players, who hanged himself in the back yard of his family home.

"It was unbelievable," the coach said. "I had never gone through anything like that. He was really a good kid. There didn't seem to be anything wrong. Russell was a guy we had voted as having the best work ethic while on the football team. And then he was gone. It hit everybody hard."

Mitch Anthony suggests: "Teammates should be taught total teamwork that includes helping each other out, even outside the court of play. Students should be encouraged to come to the coach if they recognize trouble. If teammates have a mutual commitment to look out for each other, and to go to the coach or another responsible adult when there is a problem, then the prevention process will be an effective one."

Parents can help the teenager know his limits. They do this through active listening, sharing worries or concerns, and encouraging the student to stay involved with athletics. Sometimes a personal talk with the coach, about the student's athletic potential in other sports, can be helpful.

## Social Isolation

Group social experiences are important to teenagers, along with interactions with individuals. This topic is dealt with more fully in Chapter Eight, "Social Isolation and Suicide."

Groups provide a sense of belonging and security. A lack of personal contact and group interaction results in a sense of isolation and negativism. The teenager primarily wants to "fit in," to be like everybody else.

Alan Kaplan, a psychologist and researcher at the University of Maine, found that deviant behavior or drug use was the end result of non-acceptance by peers and negative attitudes by family. Rejection by peers and parents lead to feelings of a poor self-image and loss of self-esteem. The teenager is likely to feel the stress of being left out or not important enough to be included.

Furthermore, the teenager is likely to become aware of more deviant groups, or "the wrong crowd," within the community, because the teenager is searching for ways to restore self-esteem by fitting in somewhere. As the teenager becomes integrated into these problem groups, drug-abusing behavior becomes likely, and thus a downward spiral towards suicide may begin. This happened with Kurt Brian, whose case was discussed in Chapter Three:

He moved so often for his father's military career that he fell in with a group of drug abusers.

Teachers are in a better position than parents to see how the teenager interacts in groups and may offer suggestions to the student and the parents. Teachers know that there is more than one way of doing things. They know that it is okay to be wrong and that cooperation is better than confrontation when seeking acceptance.

Parents need to be in communication with the teachers if their teenager is having problems with social integration. They should consider the teacher's suggestions, while simultaneously improving a nurturing environment at home. They can try suggesting other activities to engage the youth, relieving the teenager's fear of being isolated from peers.

## Peers As First Line of Defense

Teenagers discuss highly personal issues among themselves that they simply do not discuss with adults, even parents. These include sexual exploration, parental problems, fears, depression, and feelings of suicide, all of which are considered an inherent part of normal development. Two stories demonstrate the effect of intervention by friends.

Jason and Larry, both sixteen, listened for weeks as their friend Tom confided in them about his urge to die and how he planned to do it. The morbid talk continued steadily, until the two youths realized their friend was in danger and went to a school counselor.

Huntington Beach High School psychologist Ellen Shiro, who called the suicidal youth into her office, explained:

When all this happened, Tom was really angry at his friends, who had learned about suicide in health class. I told him it was only because his friends cared so much about him that they risked his being angry at them to come forward.

They figured out that he was in danger. He was definitely considering killing himself. His father was called in, and it turned out there was a history of suicide in the family.

After Tom received therapy, along with his family, Shiro said he was able to overcome his suicidal urges and get on with his life.

"He walked into my office a couple of weeks ago and thanked me for saving his life," she said. "He told me that now that he has his life back, he is really happy and doing really well at college."

But it isn't easy for youths to go to an adult about a friend.

Angelica was a gangly, doe-eyed girl whose life had gone from bad to worse. Her parents divorced when she was seven, and then her dad died of kidney failure when she was nine — leaving a painful void since she had never felt emotionally close to her mother. She started taking antidepressant medication at age 14, to combat feelings of hopelessness.

When she failed to get the desired results from the antidepressant, she found solace in street drugs, alcohol or sex. According to her, not having tried those things before she was 14 was her only regret.

Her life hit its lowest point when, shortly before her 17th birthday, her boyfriend told her to "drop dead." Her feelings of despair deepened. She swallowed 15 antide-pressants.

Later, she said that two thoughts had been upper-most when she tried suicide: "When am I ever going to get out of this [depression]?" and "I can't pop these pills fast enough."

She called her best friend, Carol, and left a message: "Don't worry about me any more. I love you very much."

Carol became alarmed about the ambiguous message. She had learned through a teen counseling program to recognize these as suicidal statements. She rushed over to Angelica's house. When she arrived, expecting the worst, her friend was mixing herself a cocktail. An empty bottle of antidepressants sat on the kitchen counter. Carol called the paramedics. Angelica's mother came home from the movies to find her daughter in the hospital, recovering from a suicidal overdose.

Teenagers such as Carol have a decisive advantage over adults: They are often able to save the lives of peers because of critical information friends disclose, or desper-ate telephone calls before or during a suicide attempt. The information can then be passed on to a responsible adult at school or at home.

To be effective, teenagers must act on the information they have, not just be aware of problems. Sometimes the youth fears breaking confidence, peer rejection, or looking like a tattler — all impediments to acting on behalf of a suicidal peer or friend. We must teach teens it is a heavier weight to keep certain secrets, such as the intent to com-mit suicide.

One effective program to prepare teens for this re-sponsibility has been developed by the National Suicide Education Center in Rochester, Minnesota.

The program operates on a simple concept: Within the school are individuals who will take it upon themselves to look out for the well-being of others. They attend by themselves to situations that simply require friendship, comfort, and understanding. Situations that require serious intervention or confrontation are put in the hands of a concerned and responsible adult at school or at home.

Certain students and faculty are selected to receive training on how to be a part of a network. They are selected by the student body through a survey that asks, "If you were having a serious problem, name two students and two faculty members you would most likely talk to."

The team is trained in communication skills, crisis recognition, intervention and team-building. Together, the team constitutes an actual network of caring.

The teen counseling program concept is adaptable to any team or any group setting and is based on the principle, "Care enough to do something."

Nevertheless, more and more students are bringing their problems to school. These students talk to other students, or friends before confiding in teachers, counselors, or other adults because they feel more secure, better understood by peers.

Schools must develop programs for educating personnel to deal with the problem of suicide. Our students deserve nothing less.

Chapter Six

# The Influence Of Substance Abuse

*We'd like to think that our kids don't have this problem*
*[drug abuse], but the brightest kid from the best family*
*in the community could have the problem.*

—Ralph Egers
Superintendent of Schools
South Portland, Maine

Substance abuse can lead to suicide — and, like suicide, it's an attempt to solve the problems of life. Substance abuse has been estimated to be a factor in 80 percent of all suicides involving young people. It is a serious threat to the health and well-being of children all over America.

We don't yet have the key to neutralizing this threat, but we have learned that it is not a random one: A National Institutes of Health study found that teenagers who feel connected to home, family, and school are better protected from substance abuse, violence, sexual activity, and suicide. As such, our best attempt at a solution to substance abuse and suicide is prevention.

Substance abuse allows the adolescent to escape painful psychological stimuli. Drugs initially make teenagers feel good; then it becomes necessary to keep taking them — to keep from feeling bad.

Recently, one young man described the feeling of drug addiction as being in a hole: "You can see the light (at the end of the hole), but you can't figure out how to get there." Frustration can set in because the youth can neither get off the drugs alone nor solve other problems. Like suicide, substance abuse is an attempt to solve a problem by escaping it. Drug abuse is one means of communicating one's distress before resorting to suicide.

Teenagers with a history of impulsiveness increase their risk of suicide with drug abuse. The suicidal teenager's fears, frustrations, and feelings of loneliness can develop into feelings of isolation, pain, and hopelessness due to prolonged drug abuse. The regular use of drugs affects virtually every aspect of personal and social adjustment, including the ability to cope with painful feelings.

This chapter examines reasons for substance abuse, its detrimental effects, ways to detect substance use and abuse, and solutions to substance use and abuse.

## Reasons for Substance Abuse

The reasons for drug abuse include the following:

- escape from problems or emotional pain
- substitute for an emotional need
- depression
- stress
- curiosity and experimentation
- enjoying the feeling of being high

- peer pressure
- overcoming feelings of inadequacy (e.g., shyness or being overweight, lack of acceptance)
- attempting to be different
- searching for a deeper life experience
- calming down
- ignorance
- school problems

Damon, a 22-year-old college sophomore, explains his reasons for using drugs:

I come from a dysfunctional family with an alcoholic father and a jealous mother. My parents and I cannot communicate. I feel suicidal most of the time because I am unable to control my emotions and surroundings. I use drugs as a means of escape from family problems and peer pressure.

Gerard, 19, another college sophomore, provides further insight:

The drug problems come from one's family. If the parents do not separate or divorce, they have more control over the children. Once the family's little community breaks, then it is hard, difficult for the children to lead a normal life. As an alternative, children may try drugs to relieve themselves from family problems. The whole thing comes from the experience of parents and close friends.

## Detrimental Effects of Substance Abuse

The effects of substance abuse on our youth can be devastating. Drug use and abuse impair memory, alertness, and achievement and erode the capacity of a student to perform in school. The teenager becomes unable to think clearly or act responsibly. Stewart, a high school student, describes how substance abuse affected him:

> I felt depressed and hurt all the time. I hated myself for the way I hurt my parents and treated them so cruelly and for the way I treated others. I hated myself the most, though, for the way I treated myself. I would take drugs until I overdosed, and fell further and further in school and work and relationships with others. I just didn't care anymore whether I lived or died. I stopped going to school altogether... I felt constantly depressed and began having thoughts of suicide, which scared me a lot! I didn't know where to turn....

Due to psychological dependence or addiction, drug abuse can become the center of a youth's lives. The body's craving for substances interferes with the adolescents' concentration and draws their attention from any other matters not directly related to their need to get the drug they crave.

The consequence of using drugs can last a lifetime. Drug use can destroy family ties, friendships, values, goals, and outside interests.

Family ties are sometimes broken irreparably as teenagers become more influenced by what is referred to as a "drug culture" than they are by their family. Family members are alienated when they feel they are relating to a different person than the one they knew before. The teenager now has altered self-expression, mental functioning, and thought processes, and is subject to mood swings. In addition, the teenager may resort to lying, stealing and cheating in order to acquire drugs. Ethical values plummet into a downward spiral, consistent with the degree of drug involvement. For example, the addicted youth may resort to additional poor behavior, such as prostitution or selling drugs, in order to get a personal supply of drugs.

Old friends either no longer understand or accept the drug-abusing teenager or the teenager abandons those friends, seeking relationships among those who share similar experiences with drug use.

Previous personal goals are no longer in sight. The youth's focus becomes derailed by the influence of drugs. A new lifestyle fosters mental, physical, and social deterioration. As such, there is a decline in participation in physical activities that promote good physical health and a positive outlook on life. Overall, positive activities become lacking.

Outside interests also are lacking as teenagers become increasingly concerned with their drug habit and satisfying their addiction. Further, the social deterioration that occurs makes the effort less meaningful.

The consequence of drug abuse had devastating effects on Sammy:

Sammy was the youngest of five children, three boys and two girls. His father had been killed in an automobile accident when Sammy was two years old. His mother worked long hours to support the family.

Sammy started smoking marijuana with his older brothers and neighborhood youths at age nine. By age 12, he smoked marijuana daily. His mother was aware of his behavior but did not intervene. Marijuana use progressed to drinking by age 14, and Sammy was arrested for drunkenness at age 15. Court-ordered drug counseling for Sammy did not help. Sammy died of a heroin overdose at age 19.

Sammy epitomized the young person who goes from using drugs in order to feel good, to abusing them to keep from feeling bad. Over time, the use of drugs begins to heighten the bad feelings, leading to hopelessness, helplessness and, potentially, suicide.

## Ways to Detect Substance Abuse

Action Drug Prevention Program counselors state that it is difficult to detect occasional marijuana use. Reddened eyes and a lingering sweet smell may be signs of substance abuse, but the use of eye drops, mouthwash, or burning incense easily covers these symptoms.

But heavy marijuana users often develop obvious signs such as deteriorating school performance and a loss of interest in other activities. Other signs of heavy use may be changes in friends and personality changes, including secretive behavior, or unprovoked angry flare-ups at other youths and adults.

Should drug use be suspected by someone other than a teenager's parents, it may not be easy to confront the parents, who tend to be defensive or in denial. Voicing one's concern as a question can be helpful. One should list the signs observed, explain why these are of concern, and ask the parents if they know what might be causing such behavior.

The National Federation of Parents for Drug-Free Youth has compiled a list of possible signs and symptoms of drug use. It should be noted, however, that these signs are not conclusive.

## Physical and Behavioral Symptoms

- Acting intoxicated
- "Bloodshot" or red eyes, droopy eyelids
- Imprecise eye movement
- Wearing sunglasses at inappropriate times
- Abnormally pale complexion
- Change in speech patterns and vocabulary patterns
- Frequent, persistent illness; sniffles, cough
- Change in sleep patterns such as insomnia, napping or sleeping at inappropriate times
- Repressed physical development
- Unexplained weight loss or loss of appetite
- Neglect of personal appearance, grooming
- Behavioral changes
- Unexplained periods of moodiness, depression, anxiety, irritability, hypersensitivity, or hostility
- Strongly inappropriate over-reaction to mild criticism or simple requests
- Decreased interaction and communication with others
- Preoccupation with "self," less concern for the feelings of others
- Loss of interest in previously important things such as hobbies and sports
- Loss of motivation and enthusiasm
- Lethargy, lack of energy and vitality

- Loss of ability to assume responsibility
- Need for instant gratification
- Changes in values, ideals, beliefs
- Change in friends, unwillingness to introduce friends
- School changes
- Decline in academic performance, drop in grades
- Reduced short-term memory, concentration and attention span
- Loss of motivation, interest, participation in school activities, or energy
- Frequent tardiness and absenteeism
- Less interest in participating in classes and meetings
- Sleeping in class or meetings
- Untidy appearance, dress, personal hygiene
- Slow to respond, forgetful, apathetic
- Increased discipline, behavioral problems
- Change in peer group
- Disappearance of money or items of value
- Odor of marijuana (like burnt rope) in room or clothing
- Incense or room deodorizers
- Eye drops, mouthwash
- Marijuana cigarettes (rolled and twisted at each end)
- Butt or "roach" (end of marijuana cigarette)

- Powders, seeds, leaves, plants, mushrooms
- Capsules or tablets, cigarette rolling paper
- Pipes, pipe filters, screens, strainers
- Roach clips
- Bongs, water pipes (usually glass or plastic)
- Scales, testing kits, hemostats and other equipment
- Small spoons, straws, razor blades, mirrors (for use with cocaine)
- Stash cans (soft drink, beer, deodorant, and other spray cans that unscrew at the bottom)
- Unfamiliar small containers or locked boxes
- Plastic baggies or small glass vials
- Drug-related books, magazines, comics

## Solutions to Substance Use and Abuse

The solutions to drug use and abuse are divided into preventive strategies and interventions.

### Preventive Strategies

Barry McCaffrey, Director of the Office of the National Drug Control Policy (ONDCP) has listed ten ways to drug-proof your child:

- Set a family standard on drug and alcohol use. Tell your children the rules early in grade school and repeat them often. Live by them yourself.
- Let your children know there are consequences and punishments for violating family rules, includ-

ing no car or television privileges. Make the rules clear and fair and enforce them.

- Set aside time every day to talk with your children about their lives, how they feel, and what they think. Listen and show that you care.

- Help your children establish realistic personal goals in academics, athletics, and social life. Then encourage and help them to achieve their goals.

- Know your children's friends and spend time with them. Get excited about the things your children care about. Do fun things as a family.

- Be aware. Find out the warning signs of drug abuse, from physical changes to hostility, to loss of interest in school or hobbies and watch for them.

- Talk with your children about the future. Discuss responsibilities — yours and theirs.

- Enjoy your children. Make your home a happy, positive place.

- Be a nosy parent. Ask your children questions, know where they are and who they are with. Let your children know you are asking because you love them.

- Talk to your children about drugs.

In regard to this last item, ONDCP suggests that the best thing about this subject is that you don't have to do it well. You simply have to try. If you try, your children will get the message that you care about them. They know that you understand something about the conflicts they face and that you'll be there when they need you. The alternative is to ignore the subject, which means your children are going to be listening to others who have strong opinions about the subject — those who use drugs and those who sell them.

The Office of National Drug Control Policy and Partnership for a Drug-Free America further states that when you talk to your children about drugs, it may seem as though nothing is getting through. However, this is not the case at all. The very fact that you bring it up gives it special weight.

When speaking to your children about drugs, you can start anywhere:

"Have you heard about any teens using drugs?"

"What kind of drugs?"

"How do you feel about that?"

"Why do you think young people get involved with drugs?"

"How do other teenagers deal with peer pressure to use drugs? Which approaches make

sense to you?"

"Have you talked about any of this in school?"

However you get into the subject, it's important to state exactly how strongly you feel about it. This should not be done in threatening tone, but rather, in matter-of-fact, clear language:

"Drugs are a way of hurting yourself."

"Drugs take all the promise of being young and destroy it."

"I love you too much to see you throw your life down the drain."

Finally, there are some "do's" and "don'ts" when talking about drugs with your children. The do's are as simple as speaking from the heart. The biggest don't is "Don't do all the talking." If you listen to your children, really listen and read between the lines, you'll learn a lot about what they think, about drugs, the world and you. They'll also feel heard.

If you suspect your child is on drugs, however, that's a different matter. Then you need to confront the subject directly. In the meantime, just talk to them. If you don't know much about drugs, your teenagers do. They need to know how you feel about the subject and that you care.

## Interventions

Parents are in the best position to recognize early signs of drug use in their children. If drug use is suspected, you should develop strategies:

- Devise a plan of action. Consult with school officials and other parents.

- Discuss your suspicions with your children in a calm, objective manner. Do not confront a child while he or she is under the influence of drugs.

- Impose disciplinary measures that help remove the child from those circumstances where drug use might occur.

- Seek advice and assistance from drug treatment professionals and from a parent group.

- Learn about the extent of the drug problem in the community and your children's schools.

- Meet with parents of your children's friends or classmates about the drug problem at their school. Establish a means of sharing information to determine which children are using drugs and who is supplying them.

Parents who suspect their children are using drugs often must deal with their own feelings of anger, resentment, and guilt. Frequently parents deny the evidence and postpone confronting their children. Yet, the earlier a problem is found and faced, the less difficult it is to overcome.

Chapter Seven

# The "Contagious" Effect

*"Suicide clusters probably occur much more frequently than we know. Suicide generally tends to be under-reported, in part due to concern about stigmatizing the deceased. Many such deaths are reported as accidents."*

—Mark Rosenberg, M.D.,
Centers for Disease Control, Atlanta, Georgia

Suicide among adolescents can be contagious. It can spread among vulnerable youths like a contagious disease, but without any logical pattern. One youth who commits suicide can serve as a "trigger factor" for other suicides. Suicides committed in response to the initial suicide are referred to as "cluster suicides," a chain reaction of suicides in a given area within a short period of time.

Available evidence strongly suggests that the contagion effect of suicide, sometimes referred to as a "copycat effect," is a phenomenon particular to adolescence. Teenagers who are experiencing problems at the time of another teenage suicide often see this drastic measure as a means of solving their own problems. They often identify with the teenager who committed suicide. Rosemary Rubin, of the Los Angeles Unified School District Suicide Prevention Unit, asserts that adolescents may be more susceptible to contagion factors than are young adults, as they often imitate other teens and identify with them. The following case examples illustrate the contagion phenomenon.

Nancy, 19, and Karen, 17, were best friends who lived in Illinois. They had been neighbors and classmates. Both had dropped out of school and had recently quit their jobs at restaurants. Nancy was depressed over a failed marriage. Karen was concerned that she had disappointed her parents.

The two young women were found dead in Karen's garage, apparently the victims of carbon monoxide poisoning. One was holding a rose and a stuffed animal, the other a photo album. Their method of suicide was the same as that used by four teens in New Jersey.

Those four teens, two boys named Thomas and two girls, Lisa and Cheryl, had made a suicide pact. The two girls were sisters. Three of the four were high school dropouts. Although they never said why they wanted to die, the four requested that they be "buried together." They were found in a locked car in an apartment complex after a passerby heard the car running and called police.

The mother of one of the boys said her son's best friend, Joe, had committed suicide a year earlier. Joe had jumped from a cliff overlooking the Hudson River. Following Joe's death, there were three other incidents of suicide among youths who knew each other. A total of ten adolescents committed suicide over a one-year period, after Joe jumped off the cliff.

In Arkansas, three teenagers killed themselves following the suicide of another teenager. The minister at the funeral for the first victim revealed that the three latest victims had stated that it was "too late to bring him back [the first teenager], but going with him was still our choice."

In California, Cecilia, 16, chose the railroad tracks to commit suicide. Following her suicide, two other victims chose the same gory method within a four-week period. One was a young man of 23, who had suffered the rupture of his relationship with a girlfriend. The other was a girl, 17, who drove onto the tracks ahead of an Amtrak train.

The risk factors identified in the contagion effect of suicide include depression, loss of relatives and friends, weak social support, and a previous suicide attempt.

## Depression

Depression is a common emotional reaction during adolescence. Depression is primarily a mood disorder that includes the symptoms of sadness, loneliness and apathy. There may be self-punitive wishes or a desire to escape, hide or die. Depression is essentially a negative emotion that occurs in combination with low self-esteem. Teenagers who are depressed often tell themselves, "I am inferior. I hate myself." The following is a case example of a depressed adolescent.

Dwayne was an only child. His father was a minister, and his mother was a teacher. His parents divorced when Dwayne was five years old. Dwayne excelled in many areas and was popular with peers and adults alike. However, no matter what he accomplished, he had a problem dealing with his parents' divorce.

Dwayne had been close to his father before the divorce but saw him infrequently afterwards. Dwayne always had an element of sadness that he attempted to fend off by staying busy.

His mother filed for bankruptcy in his early twenties. He suggested that she purchase insurance on his life. Upon examining the policy, Dwayne said, "Well, I guess I will have to wait two years." (The policy stipulated a two-year waiting period before a death benefit could be claimed.)

The two years passed. His girlfriend broke up with him. Three other suicides had occurred in the city the week before, all by gunshot.

On a Sunday — his mother's birthday — Dwayne took a .22 Wesson rifle and put a bullet through his brain. His suicide note read:

Dear Mom:
You are the best mother a son could have.
I love you and I love dad, too.

Dwayne

In retrospect, his mother said, "I knew he was depressed, but I did not know what to do with the information. All the signs were there."

The mother's observations are not unusual in divorce situations. The loss of a boy's father from the home during childhood often is expressed later during adolescence as suicide. More information on this is provided in Chapter Four, "Divorce and Trivorce in the family"

## Loss of Relatives and Friends

Grief work that follows the loss of a relative or a close friend is very difficult but must be done. Once a suicide occurs, and relatives or friends are cognizant of the mental and emotional pain the victim must have endured, the pain they have over the incident may be too much to bear. They may see suicide as an acceptable solution to their own pain or problems. This is illustrated in the following case.

Running buddies and cousins, Earl, 17, and Randy, 16, were home alone at Earl's house one afternoon. The two boys were inseparable; each always knew what was going on with the other. Like typical teenagers, they began to explore the house, and the two found Earl's father's pistol. Earl pretended to shoot himself through the heart. The gun discharged, killing him instantly. Realizing that he had lost his best friend, Randy took the gun and put a bullet upward through his chin, but did not die immediately. Before he lost consciousness he told his parents, "I lost my buddy. I have nothing to live for." He died the next day.

Randy's world collapsed after losing Earl, his cousin. The pain he felt was profound. As a result, the shock and disbelief phases of grieving for his best friend were too brief to enable him to begin to work through the grieving process.

Randy's suicide situation is identical to that of a star basketball player at Columbine High School. In Littleton, Colorado, where a massacre and suicides occurred, the star player there lost his best friend and fellow basketball player during the massacre. Several months later, the student killed himself, leaving a note that read, "It's too painful to go on."

## Weak Social Support

Weak social support often leads to a sad ending for teens. It is the responsibility of the family to provide emotional support for its members. Teachers, counselors, and friends are also part of the teen's support system. Quality time parents spend with their children is invaluable — listening to them, sharing their problems as well as their interests and dreams. A little encouragement goes a long way.

Teachers are like part-time parents. Their interaction and reaction with the students have a significant influence. Their observations for changes in behavior cannot be over-emphasized. In dysfunctional homes, friends, counselors and teachers may be the teenagers' sole support system. When such support is lacking, teenagers feel as if they have no foundation. This is seen in the following example:

Fifteen-year-old Lisa was the oldest of three children. Her mother was a single parent who did not look much older than Lisa because she had borne Lisa out of wedlock at a young age. The mother resented having her youth taken away by pregnancies and responsibilities. She married when Lisa was two but then blamed Lisa for the breakup of this marriage. She generally ignored Lisa and gave most of her attention to the younger children.

Lisa had low self-esteem and was socially insecure. She felt unloved and left out. She did not make friends easily. Her 13-year-old half-sister, Dana, was more socially accepted and seemed smarter.

Lisa began having problems at school. Her performance declined. She dropped out of school, feeling that her situation was hopeless. Before her suicide, she left the following note for her mother:

Dear Mom,

I can't take it any longer. You spend all your time with Dana and Eric.

I need you, too.

Love, Lisa

Lisa clearly felt alone with her problems and without caring and support from her mother. Three other recent suicides reported in the area probably had a significant impact on her decision to commit suicide.

## Previous Suicide Attempt

For many years, the psychological literature has identified previous suicide attempters as being at risk for suicide. The most plausible explanation of why teenagers commit suicide after a previous attempt is related to their developmental stage and the tendency to identify with other teens when their feelings resurface following another's suicide. Previous issues that were pushing the teenager towards the edge can also be a determinant when they have not been resolved. Veronica's case illustrates this risk factor:

Veronica, 13, lived with her mother and older brother. She was often left alone at home. Only her friend Paula visited her. She could tell Paula anything, especially how unhappy she was at home. Then Paula's mother died suddenly. Paula missed her mother desperately. She chose to commit suicide.

Veronica missed Paula. She tried committing suicide by swallowing an entire bottle of Darvocet-N, a pain medication, but survived. "I am not happy living without Paula," she said.

Unfortunately, a girl at Veronica's school committed suicide while Veronica was still pining for Paula. Three months after Paula's death, Veronica committed suicide successfully.

The suicide at Veronica's school was another reminder of the pain she was in and how much she missed her friend Paula. Suicide had resolved Paula's pain, she reasoned, so why not give it a try? A sensitive, aware parent may have been able to save Veronica by listening to her and seeking help for her. A knowledgeable school counselor may also have intervened with knowledge of both the "contagion effect" of suicide and Veronica's loss.

Chapter Eight

# Social Isolation

*The most important dynamic factor in teenage suicide is social isolation. The child frequently has no close friends to share confidences, he is chronically isolated, and he seems to have loneliness with no other alternatives.*

—Jambur Ananth, MD
*Adolescent Suicide: Contemporary Tragedy*

A sense of social isolation can have a devastating effect on the well-being of teenagers. Man is a social creature; therefore, social isolation, whether deliberate or circumstantial, is a path to loneliness, depression, and possibly suicide. The magazine editor Norman Cousins has written that all human history is an endeavor to shatter loneliness.

Adolescents appear to be more adversely affected by social isolation due to their developmental phase and their need for peer contact. In her book, *Suicide: A Preventable Tragedy*, Dorothy B. Francis states, "Almost three-fourths of the young people who make attempts on their lives have little or no social contact with others their own age.

Social isolation may appear in the form of alienation,

withdrawal, asocial behavior, inadequate or poor peer relationships, or other similar behaviors, according to Lucy Davidson in her article, "Social Isolation." Although depression is commonly seen in conjunction with social isolation, suicide may occur without depression as a factor.

Commonly identified settings and situations that cause adolescents to feel socially isolated or alienated include (1) frequently moving or changing residence, (2) changing schools, (3) going away to college, and (4) being the wrong physical size.

## Frequently Moving or Changing Residences

Relationships are difficult to establish and maintain throughout frequent changes in residence. Previously caring individuals, in the form of extended family and friends, are lost when they are left behind.

Actor Brendan Fraser relates that he experienced feelings of isolation due to frequent moves:

> I was an outsider. My family moved every two or three years and I was always the new kid. I had no real consistency in my life. In my deepest soul, I longed to be part of a community, to have a place to go. I wanted to find a way to belong but didn't know how. I wanted it so badly. That was my dream.

Brandon was the youngest of four sons. His father was frequently transferred to different cities in Europe and North America. Fraser was continually having to start over, again and again. Brandon's parents sent him to boarding school at age 13. There, he found a reprieve. At the Upper Canada College Boarding School, Brandon found his community and a sense of belonging.

The significance of boarding school was that Brandon was able to have peer friendships during the crucial teen years. Further, he was able to avoid further losses caused by being constantly uprooted and leaving friends, pets, and familiar territory behind.

Andy did not fare as well as Brandon, however. Fifteen-year-old honor student Ardy and his father moved to their current community. His heart was still in his old hometown, a small community of 5,700 people. Although there was no movie theater, only a one-room library, and few opportunities, still, Andy felt he had friends there and was loved.

His father, however, wanted him to be near their family, so they moved, stopping briefly for a while to live with Andy's grandparents. The father, feeling the he could earn more in another city, decided to move to a location near San Diego. He allowed Andy to go back and visit with friends over the summer.

Andy cried when he realized his summer vacation was coming to a close. School was about to begin in Santee, California, but Andy told the woman he called Mom, "I don't want to go back!" Several days before school started, Andy was back home in San Diego.

Immediately upon enrolling, the name-calling started: "Albino" because he was pale, "Ethiopian" because he was slender and of slight build, "gay" because his voice was not deep. He had been beaten up because of his new haircut, had eggs thrown at his apartment, had his sneakers taken, and his homework thrown into the garbage. Not only were the bullies consistently targeting Andy, but other students who were picked on themselves also picked on him.

Andy's friends berated and taunted him because he refused to defend himself against teasing and bullying. Andy responded by saying, "I'll show you one day. It'll happen. You'll see." Andy told his friends how difficult things had become for him. "If I could just hide out for awhile."

The school punished him for being tardy. His grades dropped, and he failed several courses. Andy would have to attend summer school and would not be able to spend the summer in his former hometown.

One Monday morning, after the usual routine of meeting with his other teenage student friends, Andy strolled across the small quad into the boys' restroom. The quad was a gathering place for students before class and during breaks. Minutes after Andy went into the restroom, several "Pop! Pop!" sounds were heard. No one could identify the muffled, firecracker-like sounds.

Right there in the quad, students began to fall. Other students were tripping over each other, running into trees, screaming as they ran for their lives. Blood flowed on the ground like water. There was Andy, with a wild grin on his face, firing indiscriminately at students in the quad. "Oh, my God! Oh, my God!" some students were saying as they ran for safety.

In the restroom, Andy was reloading his revolver when an off-duty officer cornered him. Andy was ordered to drop the gun, which he did. Upon instructing other officers to check the stalls for accomplices, Andy meekly replied, "It's only me." Two students lay dead in the restroom.

At Juvenile Hall sometime later, Andy stated that he had 40 rounds of ammunition. His plan was to use 39 at school . He would save the last one, run away, and kill himself.

Andy's parents were divorced, and his support system was in his old hometown. Moving away was devastating for him, as it can be with many high school students. Moving during a teenager's high school years is strongly discouraged. Andy felt like an unwelcomed outsider, both at school and in the community.

School problems are consistently mentioned in the psychological profiles of teenagers who commit or attempt suicide. While school can be a place where adolescents meet each other and develop friendships, loneliness or a feeling of being alone can occur if a student is not socialized into a group or does not have friends.

The most poignant example of social isolation, in the form of alienation and asocial behavior, was demonstrated by two high school students in the Columbine Colorado High School massacre in 1999. The youths' outsider status led not only to their own self-destruction, but also to the devastation of many other lives. The two loners must have been terrified at the thought of going through life with such intense feelings of isolation. They converted the anger they felt at being rejected into revenge against others.

Drs. Lucy Davidson and Markku Linnoila in *Risk Factors for Youth Suicide* identify social integration as a risk factor for suicide. Social integration refers to a binding of people together in a collective body, with which individuals identify and incorporate into their own identity. The two students at Columbine, Eric Harris and Dylan Klebold, were known at school as part of the "Trench Coat Mafia," a clique of "geeky" loners. Teachers, reading their gloomy papers and watching their video with dark destructive messages, had no insight into how troubled these two boys were.

One of Dylan's teachers did speak with his parents about a story of a violent nature. The father told the teacher, "It is a just a story," and he did not see why they were "making such a big deal of it." Many observers believe that such aloofness on the part of the parents of Eric Harris and Dylan Klebold meant that the boys were essentially isolated in their own homes. Unable to communicate at home and rejected at school and in the community, they came to see destruction followed by death as a satisfactory solution.

Kevin Dwyre, a school psychologist, in referring to Eric and Dylan, stated, "What happens right before the eyes of grown-ups, parents and teachers — but not necessarily within their range of vision — is that the situation gave the kids the permission to do things they had no business doing."

Although they had not recently changed residences, the suicides of Eric Harris and Dylan Klebold demonstrate "egoism," or what French sociologist Emile Durkheim identified as excessive individuation and too little social integration with the larger student body. Davidson and Linnoila state that many experts attribute the increase in suicide and violence to increasing divorce rates and the diminishing importance of religion and moral values. Others suggest that large, impersonal high schools make it difficult for teenagers to find a sense of self-worth and to establish friendships.

On a makeshift memorial of crosses erected to victims of the massacre, including two for Eric and Dylan, visitors left a small message on theirs. "Your lives were lost long before this ever happened. Shame on all of us for never noticing."

## Going Away to College

College-bound students are not always able to make an adequate adjustment when they move away from the support of family and friends. The movie, *After Jimmy*, is a compelling story of an 18-year-old honor student who commits suicide while attempting to make the transition to college. Initially, Jimmy had been absorbed in his schoolwork, which probably protected him from the isolation he felt. His social interaction was minimal, and his relationship with his parents was characterized by blocked communication.

Jimmy began failing in school. He turned his papers in late and dropped out of the soccer team. His college application was never mailed, and he never told his parents about his insensitive principal. Jimmy was seen crying on the school lawn. In a typical suicidal gesture, he gave a favorite jacket to his friend, Garth. Here, social isolation was coupled with a suicidal expression, the giving away of his jacket. The two factors appearing together significantly predict a risk for suicide.

Initially, his mother was in denial: "He was happy! He danced with his grandmother. Ask anyone! Why would he want to kill himself?" Later, his mother started to doubt her perceptions.

Jimmy had kept it all inside. Along with constant difficulties, such as low self-esteem, he had feelings of guilt and emptiness. He also felt ashamed and did not want his parents to think badly of him or to let them down. Jimmy was found hanging in the garage at seventeen and one-half years. His parents blamed each other for his death.

Suicide attempts are significantly high among first-year college students who do not have the skills to integrate themselves into college social life. It behooves parents to be aware and to stay in frequent contact with their young person, communicating love and support.

Loneliness and the desire for social acceptance are often found among obese teenagers. Monique, a 14-year-old, felt she was "too fat and ugly to live." She started throwing up after every meal to feel better about herself. She suffered from low self-esteem and stopped talking to her mother. "I feel separate from the other girls," Monique stated. She wanted to be slender and pretty like the other girls at school. It was not to be. Monique died of anorexia.

Thirteen-year-old Laura was teased and called names at school. Teachers did nothing to stop the behavior. In addition to the name-calling, other teenagers threw rocks at her. Laura began cutting her wrist. "I can't remember what happy feels like," she said. "I feel so alone. I am too ugly to live."

While moving from one school district to another is not recommended for high school students, this is an instance in which it would have been helpful for Laura to have a fresh start. She needed to be in a place where she was more likely to be accepted. Laura was found by her mother in her closet dead from hanging.

## Being the Wrong Physical Size

Physical size that doesn't fall within the "normal" range is a source of pain and isolation for many youths. The teenager wants desperately to "fit in" and be accepted. It is extremely important at this age for teenagers not to have negative attention drawn to themselves. Such attention can come from being too big, too small, too short, or too tall.

## Summary

For teenagers, social acceptance is extremely important. Social isolation and alienation can result from frequently moving or changing residence, a lack of acceptance at school, going away to college, or differences in physical size or appearance. Parents, teachers, and counselors need to be aware of these risk factors and to pay attention to any symptoms of social isolation. Soloman Snyder, in *Teenage Depression and Suicide,* asserts, "the family that can provide communication, love and support for its members is, in Christopher Losch's phrase, 'a haven in a heartless land.'"

Chapter Nine

# Rejection And Revege

*Suicide may be viewed by the adolescent as a triumph over a world that has rejected him.*

—George Howe Colt
*The Enigma of Suicide*

Rejection is the feeling of being unwanted, alienated or isolated from another person, family, or group — such as a school. The pain of rejection pushes many adolescents to suicide.

Samuel Klagsburg, a psychiatrist with expertise in adolescent suicide, comments that "adolescents who depend on others for a sense of self-worth may find a reason to live in someone or something else. They put all their eggs in one basket — a sport, a grade, a person — which then becomes all-important. Often that reason may be a boyfriend or girlfriend. If that relationship becomes tremendously overvalued, it becomes the foundation of the person's life. 'If the person loves me, I am okay.' But if that goes, it's as if everything goes — because there's nothing else to bank on.

Often suicide is an attempt to punish the person who failed them. It may be that a social relationship the teenager initiated has resulted in frustration, humiliation, shame, or anger. When this happens, adolescents sometimes experience a "failed self."

Suicidiologist Robert Litman points out:

> Sometimes suicide may be, paradoxically, an attempt to preserve self-image. I believe that suicide has a lot to do with the ideal — often unconscious — that one has of oneself based on early relationships. Suicidal people tend to believe that if they do not live up to this model, their lives must be a total failure. Often, then, they kill themselves in order to preserve the ideal, to save the flag, save the halo — in addition to punishing the failed self. It's a breeding concept for suicide, because many people think it's either my way or no way, and if it's no way, it's suicide.

Rejection can be experienced from one's family as well as from other sources. In his book, *Adolescent Suicide,* William Kirk notes that suicidal adolescents perceive their parents to be much more rejecting than non-suicidal adolescents do. When families experience turmoil and do not have the communication skills needed to resolve conflicts in helpful ways, a painful atmosphere is created, which can contribute to the incidence of adolescent suicide.

The experience of rejection hinders further communication. The youth, afraid of further rejection, becomes unable to express thoughts or feelings. The opportunity to share feelings and thoughts with others, and thereby seek help, becomes lost. This is compounded by the fact that, in general, teenagers find it difficult to ask for support.

According to Richard Bedrosian, a cognitive psychologist,

> Teenagers lack the mental health resources to cope with losses, and find it hard to ask for and receive the support from others that nurtures adults through similar situations or stressful periods. In addition, the adolescent tends to see rejection or disapproval from others as reflections of personal worth (or worthlessness).

In some cases, punishment, blame, and revenge not only include suicide, but also homicide before the suicide occurs. A suicide of rejection and revenge can involve two people, such as two young lovers, or it can bring about the suicide and massacre that occurred at Columbine High School in 1999. Explicit revenge however, does not always accompany rejection.

Presented here are two examples of the suicide of rejection. Both cases can be understood as having a sense of "failed self" at their core.

## Aliso

Like many teenagers, 16-year-old Aliso suffered from what he perceived as a devastating rejection and loss; his girlfriend broke up with him. He felt rejected. His mood changed, and he withdrew from his friends. He warned the friends about his intention to kill himself. Then, a few days later, shortly before his photography class, Aliso went home and took a weapon from a locked chest belonging to his father. During the class, Aliso stood up before the girl who had rejected him and the rest of his class, placed the gun under his chin, and fired a single shot.

## The Relationship Between Suicide and Homicide

Suicide and homicide are similar acts of violence. According to Dr. Saul B. Wilen of the Team-Based Suicide Prevention center in San Antonio, Texas, "A close relationship exists between suicide and violence against others."

Dr. Joyce Brothers adds, "There is rage and anger in all of us." Many of the factors that cause the pain and anger that lead to suicide also cause the rage and anger that lead to homicide. It is difficult to predict whether an individual will choose homicide in addition to suicide; this depends on the individual's perspective. If one's problems are seen as the work of others, then one may take action against them. If one sees oneself as inadequate, then suicide is the result. If both together are perceived as causing the problem, then both suicide and homicide are likely to occur.

## Victor

Victor and Rosa Maria had been seeing each other for six months. Although Victor was only 16 years old and she was 14, Rosa Maria was three months' pregnant by Victor. Her mother felt that Victor was a bad influence on her. He had tried to punch her, but his fist missed, and he struck a wall instead. Rosa had told her friends that Victor did not want her talking to them, and she began to ditch school. Her mother convinced her to stop seeing Victor and told Rosa Maria that her family would take care of the baby.

On a Friday night, Victor asked a friend to give him a ride to Rosa Maria's house to return some mementos. Rosa Maria was home with her family when Victor knocked on the door. Rosa Maria went outside to exchange the mementos they had given each other over their six-month relationship. Rosa Maria's mother followed her and urged her back inside.

Victor asked Rosa Maria if the baby she was carrying was his. Her mother responded that he did not have to worry about it. At that point, Victor pulled a handgun and shot at the mother, but missed. Rosa Maria tried to push him away. Victor fired again, hitting Rosa Maria in the head, killing her. He shot her mother several more times before leaving the house, also killing her.

Victor was later found in the street nearby, dead of a self-inflicted gunshot wound. His family said he had never shown any signs that he was capable of hurting himself or others.

## Recommendations

Since it is highly unlikely that revenge will occur without rejection, parents, teachers, and counselors need to stress the importance of communication. More important than stressing communication, parents, teachers, and counselors need to make themselves available to adolescents and to listen in a non-judgmental way.

Parents also need to be aware that rejection and isolation of a new student is common and can cause the adolescent a great deal of distress. It is highly recommended that moving a teenager be postponed, if at all possible, until after graduation from high school. If moving is necessary, parents, along with counselors and teachers, need to find ways to help the student make a satisfactory adjustment. A "New Student" program is recommended for schools to help make a satisfactory transition.

If counselors hear of, or teachers observe, students being picked on — especially students new to the school — they need to have ready responses to support and help the adolescent. All too often, teachers choose to ignore the plight of the student who is picked on or who has experienced rejection. Parents, teachers, and counselors must take a more active role in looking out for and helping such adolescents. A school mediator can help when bullying occurs.

Chapter Ten

# Suicide And Gender

*One of the most perplexing facts about suicide is that females attempt suicide more, but more males succeed in ending their lives.*

—Susan J. Blumenthal, M.D.
Deputy Assistant Secretary for Health


In the United States, we see gender differences in adolescent suicide rates, with females more likely than males to engage in suicidal behavior, but less likely to die as a result of a suicidal act. The Centers for Disease Control and Prevention report that "females were significantly more likely than males to report that they had thought seriously about attempting suicide, made a suicide plan, or attempted suicide one or more times during the twelve months preceding the survey."

Although this book is about adolescent suicidal behavior in the United States, it is interesting to note how the patterns of adolescent suicide differ by gender worldwide. In the Unites States, the ratio of male suicides to female suicides is 5:1. A 1990 World Health Organization reported similar findings among countries reporting to them.

According to popular myth, females die for "love" and males die for "glory." Females become suicidal over problems in relationships with males when they are "discarded by a lover or husband." Suicidal behavior in females is viewed as dependent, immature, weak, and even hysterical. Silvia Sara Canetto, a researcher at Colorado State University, Fort Collins, found that the idea that females succumb to suicide for love has a long tradition in Western culture.

Also, according to prevalent mythology, love and longing for a relationship are not primary motivations for suicide among men. The phrase "he died for glory" refers to performance, pride, and independence. Males are suicidal when their self-esteem and independence are threatened.

Canetto, however, presents a different perspective: "No matter how potent a suicide is made up to be, a suicide always implies resignation and defeat. In Western cultures, men are not supposed to fall to defeat; they are supposed to win and be in control of others. Thus, claiming victory through suicide is not very convincing."

Gender differences in suicide rates are also believed to occur because males use more lethal weapons when they attempt suicide. Nationwide, firearms and explosives are the most common methods used in suicide attempts. Boys are much more likely than girls to use guns or explosives in suicide attempts; girls are more likely to use poison.

Culture may be a plausible explanation for gender differences in suicide rates. For example, Latina females were found to make significantly more suicide attempts than Caucasian or African-American females. Further, Latinos, both male and female, make the most suicide attempts overall. It should be emphasized here that the actual number of suicide attempts is higher in Latinos, but completed suicides in Latinos are lower than those among Caucasians or African-Americans.

One commonly held notion about suicide and gender is the notion that more male homosexuals commit suicide than females. Lesbianism is believed to be more acceptable or easier to "keep in the closet" for females. There are no hard statistics to confirm either belief, and more information is needed in this area of suicide.

Chapter Eleven

# Sociocultural Aspects And Race

*Culture not genetic, it is learned and changes over time. It is not only learned in the family, but in institutions of society.*

—Bill Mauer
Associate professor of Anthropology,
University of California, Irvine

In America, culture, society, and race have been identified as important factors associated with suicide. While each of these factors is critically important, the interaction between them in an individual's immediate environment is highly complex - sometimes inexplicable.

The United States population is comprised of five major cultural groups:

- Native Americans/Alaskan Natives
- Asian/Pacific Islanders
- Black/African-Americans
- Hispanic/Latino-Americans
- European/White Americans

Within each major cultural group are different ethnic groups whose communities may vary widely, based on their immigration history, location, place of birth, length of stay in the United States, education, socioeconomic factors, and other factors as well. Enormous differences may exist between communities that are ethnically similar in membership — and might look the same to outsiders.

## Dynamics and Trends of Suicide

Western states have shown the highest suicide rates.
Rates are lower in the country than in the city.
Rates vary from city to city as well as within the cities themselves.
Neighborhoods with shifting populations and wealthy sections have the highest suicide
rates.
Within cities, suicide rates differ among ethnic groups.
New immigrants have rates
closer to their homelands than to those of their adopted country.
October is the cruelest month, twelve percent above the suicide rate.
Saturday is the least popular day of the week.
Monday is the most popular.
Culture affects dynamics and trends of suicide.

## Culture and Social Phenomena

Suicide statistics are often reported in racial categories. When considering cultural differences as factors in suicide, it's important to be aware of the limitations on our knowledge.

Anthropologist Edward Hall commented in *The Silent Language*, "It is almost impossible to communicate cultural understanding to anyone who has not lived through the experience."

In addition, Hall concluded that culture controls behavior in deep and persisting ways, many of which are outside of individual awareness and, therefore, beyond conscious controls. Consequently, culture cannot be taught in the same way language is taught. No constant elemental units of culture have as yet been satisfactorily established. However, each culture has its own beliefs about such concepts as personal space, social organization, and time.

As stated previously, "culture" means everything that is socially learned and shared by a society, even though Hall failed to find these constant units. Culture-related phenomena have been shown to be relevant to different rates of suicide in different countries, for example, those of Scandinavia: Denmark, Sweden, and Norway.

In Denmark and Sweden, where suicide rates are high, children are encouraged to be dependent on the mother and to suppress aggressive feelings. Failure to meet these goals arouses guilt. Emphasis is put on competition, performance, and achievement. Parents' expectations for performance are intense and rigid, so success or failure has a life-or-death meaning. Youths engage in self-hatred for failure but are taught not to express their emotions, so they react by withdrawal and detachment. Suicide in these countries is generally performance-based, triggered by a failure to live up to perceived expectations.

Norway has lower suicide rates. Family ties are stronger, as are ties to neighborhoods, social clubs, and church. These close bonds apparently form because mothers are warm and emotionally involved with their children without having rigid expectations. Norwegian youths are better able to express their anger and frustrations in ways short of suicide.

According to the great sociologist Durkheim, suicide has social origins. Peter Hamilton, in *Emile Durkheim: Critical Assessments*, wrote that Durkheim considered the family one of the most important social institutions. Durkheim also believed in the institution of marriage, although he stated that marriage itself suffers from divorce and, thus, has a destructive influence on the family. He concluded, "The function of marriage is to regulate passion."

In 1895 Durkheim wrote that he had "achieved a clear view of the essential role played by religion in social life." He believed that when the level of social integration became higher, the level of suicide became lower in Norwegian society. He used religion as an indicator of social integration and said that Protestantism is a highly individualized faith, allowing a great deal of latitude in behavior.

Durkheim judged Catholicism to be a faith much more regulated by highly detailed rules, and, thus, explained the lower incidence of suicide among Catholics than among Protestants. He gave evidence for this view from his findings on Catholics and Protestants in Spain, Germany, and France. According to Durkheim, Protestants commit suicide more than Catholics and Catholics more than Jews.

He further analyzed the inability of traditional social structures to provide the basis of social integration as follows:

1) The family is an insufficiently encompassing social structure.

2) Religious structures are similarly too limited in their scope and too much oriented toward the sacred.

3) Government is too bureaucratic and hence too re-
mote from the individual.

# Five Major Cultural Groups

## European/White Americans

American culture is based primarily on white European cultural norms. White Americans come from many
different heritages: German, Irish, Italian, French, Polish,
Dutch, Scottish, Swedish, British, Portuguese, Russian,
and others. According to Judith Katz, in *The Sociopolitical
Nature of Counseling,* many white Americans find it difficult to identify with the culture of their ethnic origin.

Katz stresses that as a result of this, white culture "is
so interwoven in the fabric of everyday living that whites
cannot step outside and see their beliefs, values, and behavior as creating a distinct cultural group." She defines
American white culture as "the synthesis of ideas, values,
beliefs coalesced from descendants of white ethnic groups
in the United States.

### Values/Practices

The traditional white American family is predomi-
nantly nuclear, consisting of a husband, wife, and their
children. The husband is generally the breadwinner.
Three-generation families are uncommon, but a degree
of closeness does exist among generations, with a willingness to help each other stand on his/her own two feet.
The number of female-headed households is increasing,
however, because of adoptions, divorce, and a preference
for single parenthood.

Verbal communication is linear and direct. Great emphasis is put on eye contact. Comfortable personal space for conversation is two feet. A greeting consists of a handshake. Much culture is communicated non-verbally.

### Individualism/Social Interaction

Nelson Hultberg, in *Individualism Strengths and America*, writes: "One of [white] America's trademarks is the concept of individualism. White Americans believe that they are responsible for their own lives and possess powers within themselves to overcome any obstacle."

Responsibility for choice is put on the individual as well. Katz says that "Rugged Individualism" is a major component of white American culture. The individual, not the family, is the primary unit for action. Independence and autonomy are highly valued and rewarded.

White Americans are generally action-oriented. They believe they must always do something about a situation, as in the proverb: "The squeaky wheel gets the grease."

Material possessions are considered benefits of hard work. Economic possessions, credentials, titles, and positions are considered measures of status and power.

Hall emphasized white Americans' obsession with time:

> We look ahead and are almost entirely oriented backward, it is rarely to take pleasure in the past itself, but usually to assess the prognosis for success.

Thus, time is a valuable commodity that can be saved, lost and wasted. Deadlines and schedules are taken seriously. Promptness is valued. For example, my outpatient clinic supervisor was nothing short of a military drill sergeant. A group of us student nurses arrived at 6:57 for a 7

A.M. assignment. She ranted and raged, saying we should have been there at 6:50. All of us were referred to our advisors for counseling.

## Suicide

According to the National Center for Injury Prevention and Control (NCIPC), in 1997 white males accounted for seventy-two percent of all suicides. Together, white males and white females accounted for over ninety percent of all suicides for that year. These statistics are part of a long-standing trend in the United States. The specific reasons are not clear. Since a large number of white suicides are in the 20-to-24-year-old college-age range, pressures to be successful may be too great. Personal aspirations and self-expectations may be too high.

Richard Seiden, a professor of psychology at the University of California at Berkley, advises,

> I am not saying people should live in poverty and suffer discrimination, but it seems the people with the most to live for seemingly, which is white males, have the hardest road. No racial difference is found in the genes. The problem seems to be one of class. People in the upper classes all over the world have a higher suicide rate.

Sociocultural aspects leading to suicide are complex, but two that appear to cause problems for white American adolescents are a success orientation and the emphasis on individual responsibility to find a solution to a problem in the foreseeable future. If one is stuck in the present, the future is difficult to see. Time is an essential element in suicide. Religion appears to have an influence on suicide rates.

# Native Americans and Alaska Natives

Native Americans and Alaska Natives accounted for sixty-four percent of all U.S. suicides from 1979 to 1992. For those years the Native American adolescent had the highest suicide rate of any cultural group. The reason cited most often was the effect of a dual culture. Cultural barriers such as ethnocentrism, cultural relativism, cultural blindness, stereotyping, prejudice, and racism have also been problems.

Michael D. Resnick, an epidemiologist, wrote in the *Journal of the American Medical Association*: "This is the most devastated group of adolescents in the United States."

Native Americans and Alaska Natives are the smallest of the cultural groups or ethnic minorities in the United States. They reside in each of the fifty states, but over half of them are concentrated in the Western portion of the country: Oklahoma, Arizona, California, and New Mexico.

Teresa Lafromboise and Delores Subia Bigfoot's *Journal of Adolescence* article, "Cultural and Cognitive Considerations in the Prevention of American Indian Adolescent Suicide," provides valuable insights into the problem.

According to Lafromboise and Bigfoot, Native American adolescent suicide "reflects the hopelessness of trapped and imprisoned souls. Suicide may be construed as the ultimate act of freedom."

Alienation and depression that often precede suicide are precipitated by cultural idiosyncrasies. For example, suicides among the Hopi Indians occur more frequently among adolescent males whose parents have entered into marriage outside the clan or village. These marriages are not acceptable to the highly complex, ritualistic religion and to the social structure of the tribe. As a result, the offspring of these marriages are frequently deprived of their ceremonial heritage, kinship affiliation, and approval of the extended family, factors that might help to counteract the self-destructive behavior that often emerges during puberty.

Native Americans' perceptions of death emphasize self-control over preparation for death rather than control of its occurrence. Death is seen as merely a part of the natural pattern of life events, as inevitable as changing seasons. Native Americans express gratitude to God for having been allowed to exist at all. Fearing death less was found to be a prevailing factor in those more serious about acting on suicidal impulses.

It is interesting to find that Native Alaskan culture both recognizes and respects an individual's right to actively participate in all phases of the dying process, while Native American adolescents who attempt suicide complain about the cultural expectation of their independent decisions. Suicide for Native American youths becomes a viable alternative to feeling helpless and overwhelmed.

Cultural values reflect what Native Americans want or prefer. Many experience conflict when they attempt to internalize alien values of the dominant society, or they seek out opportunities to practice the traditional role relationships necessary to maintain traditional values.

For Native Americans, family has a broader meaning than just the nuclear family of father, mother, and children of the dominant American culture. The extended family is an integral part of Native American life. Family is so important that to be without relatives is to be considered poor. The extended family shares a common dwelling and assumes responsibility for members. Native Americans value the wisdom and guidance of their elders, and their society is traditionally matriarchal.

Communication is usually non-assertive and retiring. Silence is tolerated more easily than by other people in Western society. Emotions are not shown.

### Individualism and Social Interaction

The Native American highly respects harmony with nature, and respect is also a part of social interactions. There is generally a group orientation but with individual goals. Native Americans do not like to call attention to themselves in a group, but they value hospitality.

Concept of time includes a cultural interpretation with a three-point range that includes the past, present and future. Generally, Native Americans are viewed as present oriented, but some are perceived as facing toward the past or present. In sharp contrast to white American culture, in Native American culture time is not rigidly structured, and there is always enough of it. Native Americans have little or no future orientation. A clock does not dictate life. Time is viewed as a continuum without a beginning or end.

In the past, Native Americans were not concerned with materialism and success. This lack of concern is currently changing, but sharing is still more important than accumulation. Building a "nest egg" is not a concern, as Indians usually work to meet present needs.

Religion, as a rule, is limited to myths, legends, the supernatural, and spirits. Values and beliefs are intrinsic in Native Americans' everyday lives. If present, Christian beliefs are often coupled with more traditional spiritual beliefs.

## Cultural Beliefs

The Native American belief in reincarnation and in reciprocal influences between human and spirit worlds characterizes death as an extension of earthly life into a spiritual realm. As an example, the Hopi people attribute death and illness to witchcraft, personal sins, misconduct, spiritual imbalance, and certain supernatural experiences. The belief in reincarnation implies a continuous process of striving for perfection in humans.

The belief in reciprocity of influence between the human and spirit worlds may reduce some fear surrounding death since the dead are thought to remain in interaction with the living and retain concern for the living.

The belief in both reincarnation and reciprocity between the human and spirit worlds may act as a coping mechanism when one is contemplating whether or not to self-destruct. Also, many believe that life is a gift to be accepted and not to be disrespected, and this belief might help to keep self-destructive impulses under control.

Identity Diffusion in Native American Adolescents

Problems of adolescence are more complex for Native American youths than for those in the dominant culture. As the transition from childhood to adulthood begins, adolescents are confronted with the reality of being stranded between two cultures. They desire to retain the cultural heritage and nurturance of their people, but there are ambiguous messages from the dominant society that expects them to acculturate, yet fails to assimilate or accept them.

There is no single definition of "Native American" since Native Americans are often considered "Native" for some purposes but not for others. A specific group of youths who are at risk are those adopted by white families because they feel rootless.

### Frequency of Loss

Apparently there are problems specific to Americans Indians. Frequent losses, such as having been cared for by more than one significant-other care giver during developing years, having been cared for by primary caregivers with numerous arrests, having desertion or divorce among primary care givers, having been arrested at a significantly early age, having suffered an arrest in the twelve-month period preceding death, and having attended boarding school before the ninth grade seem to increase the possibility of suicide. These variables represent separation, loss of loved ones, or loss of face.

### Hardship Pervasiveness

In Native American communities, hardships are pervasive because of continuous periods of mourning within close-knit extended families due to suicide, homicide, and accidental deaths; coupled with the daily hassles of long-term poverty, social and political tensions, unavailability of employment, and underachievement in education. All of these hardships undermine the adolescent's coping efforts. Adolescents more than adults might feel desperation over the threats and disturbances in their lives.

Some experts attribute the high rates of substance abuse and broken homes within the Native American population to family disruptions and other kinds of uprooting that occurred during the last two centuries.

Culturally Based Suicide Prevention and Treatment

Programs have been developed to stem the tide of adolescent suicides on the reservations. Young people are made aware of ways to cope with adversity by elders and volunteers who help with coping strategies. A current update is needed to analyze the effectiveness of these interventions.

Recent developments, such as the benefit of revenue from casinos, will provide additional support for better education and job opportunities, as well as fostering a sense of self-reliance and enhancing self-esteem.

Culturally competent professionals — such as teachers and school counselors on reservations as well as in the general population — and more sensitivity in the dominant culture will help young Native Americans to avoid self-destructive behavior.

## Asians and Pacific Islanders

Asian and Pacific Island people are not homogeneous. The largest Asian groups in the United States are Chinese, Filipino, Japanese, Asian Indian, Korean, and Vietnamese. The largest Pacific Islander groups are Hawaiian, Samoan, Tongan, and Guamanian. Those born in the United States have adopted the cultural values of American society and of educated Asians.

The Asian/Pacific family is extended. Children commonly live with their parents until they marry. Asian American cultures convey their caring for each other in less demonstrative ways than in the dominant culture. Parents expect children to follow their guidance and rarely encounter "back-talk." A sense of interconnectedness exists rather than individualism. More information on Asian-American culture is needed.

### Individualism and Social Interaction

In Asian communities the individual is recognized as

unique and is recognized-according to age, role, status, education, wealth and wisdom. A kind of "structural order" exists, which allows the individual to know his or her place in the family and community. The person makes an effort not to bring shame to the family. It is also important not to cause unpleasantness in social relationships.

The main responsibility for a child's socialization rests with the parents, but extended families are also actively involved in helping the child to become a respected member of society.

### Materialism and Success

Accomplishments, correct behavior and status are all measures of success for Asian Pacific persons. There is a sense of family and group orientation and interdependence, so that sharing, borrowing, and lending are important ways of life for many.

### Concept of Time

Time is generally related to events. Those events which involve family or emergencies take priority over events that are not personal. Time is flexible; there is always enough time.

Among Asians and Pacific Islanders, male suicides fall below those of whites, Native Americans, and blacks, but above Hispanics. However, the suicide rate slightly increases for females, making them second to white females, according to a report by the Department of Health and Human Services.

Not enough literature is available on suicides of adolescents of Asian and Pacific Islander extraction. Robert Roberts, a researcher on teenage mental health at the University of Texas, writes, "Too little is known about suicidal behavior in Asian Americans and some other minorities," especially those from Cambodia and Vietnam.

Although Asian Americans are frequently lumped together into one monolithic group, differences in cultural responses to suicide do exist. As an example, Ford Koromoto, executive director of the National Asian Pacific American Families Against Substance Abuse, says that the Japanese culture has historically accepted suicide as an honorable alternative to shame or loss of face. On the other hand, suicide is discouraged in Chinese society even though it is not considered a sin as in western religions. "The act of suicide has been viewed as a shameful act and brings dishonor to a family but it can also be interpreted as an honorable act," writes Julia Shiang, professor of psychology at the Pacific Graduate School in Palo Alto.

According to Shiang, because Chinese society emphasizes the good of the group over the needs of the individual, suicide is seen as a social rather than a psychological act.

Filipinos, the majority of whom are Catholic, are less tolerant of suicide and consider it an unforgivable sin.

Generally, there is no evidence that acculturation and assimilation tension have caused the "caught between cultures" syndrome in Asians.

## African-Americans

African-Americans are people of African ancestry and people from the West Indies and the Caribbean (Belize, Jamaica, Trinidad, the Dominican Republic, Haiti, Puerto Rico, and other countries). Few, if any, American-born African-Americans are of pure African descent.

At one time, African-Americans comprised the largest ethnic minority of the four groups in the United States, about twelve-and-one-tenth percent of the population. Like the other four major groups, African-Americans are heterogeneous. Members come from different countries and have different cultures, languages, and dialects. Native and foreign-born African-Americans are included. Values listed may not apply to all African-Americans as with other racial groups. In other words, every African-American does not think like every other African-American as generally assumed. It is this precise assumption that American-born African-Americans fight against daily.

## Black/African-American Values and Practices

### Family

American-born African-Americans value both the nuclear family and an extended family. The extended family has been part of the African-American experience since the days of slavery. The extended family is important in providing a source of emotional, moral, and other support during difficult times. Children who were often reared by relatives in extended family homes, but, today, they are more likely to be found in foster homes today.

An increasing number of African-American females are found parenting alone. In 1997 the Census Bureau reported that females headed forty-five percent of African-American households. Family ties are still close, even though physical closeness and support are less readily available due to scattered employment.

Many African-American professionals believe that family patterns continue to be influenced by the negative and lingering effects of the slavery years, when families were broken up and torn apart. Since that time a lack of education and job opportunities for black men, racism, and discrimination have not helped matters.

## Communication Style

Non-verbal communication predominates among African-Americans. Strangers may be greeted with a handshake or ritual handclasp. Relatives and friends are greeted with hugs. Entire side conversations may be conducted with eye movements, facial gestures, and body language such as shrugging the shoulders. Many uneducated Southern African-Americans generally avoid direct eye contact. Silence may indicate a lack of interest.

## Individualism/Social Interaction

Respect for elders is stressed. Adults are usually not called by their first names, as that would be considered a sign of disrespect. Most African-Americans have a social orientation, as is demonstrated by the large numbers in helping professions such as social work and teaching. However, according to psychologist Dr. Sandra Cox, more youths are now buying into the dominant cultural notion of "rugged individualism," to their detriment.

## Education

Many African-Americans regard education as the doorway to the European American way of life: acculturation and assimilation. Some generally possess a strong sense of self-determination and a belief that success can be achieved through hard work. Others fear failure and lack motivation for both education and work.

## Concept of Time

Time is flexible for most. Those who have acculturated

have become more strict and less flexible. When an event fails to begin on time, one is likely to hear, "They are operating on colored people's time, CPT." The flexible time schedule for meetings and events allows the participants to relax and socialize before starting an event.

### Religion

The church, a community center, has always been the major institution in not only sustaining survival and instilling hope for African-Americans, but also teaching values and culture. Many African-American youths are currently unaware of the role the church has played in the lives of African-American people in the United States.

A 1998 report by the Centers for Disease Control and Prevention suggests that suicide is an "important and growing problem" among young African-Americans. The problem may be linked to the upward mobility of the African-American middle class.

While no conclusive cause was cited for the rise in the suicide rate of black teenagers, more African-Americans are being reared in upwardly mobile families, where more of them might be experiencing stresses created in the environment. The CDC report further states: "These youths may adopt the coping behaviors of the larger society in which suicide is more commonly used in response to depression and hopelessness."

Harvard psychiatrists Alvin Poussaint and Amy Alexander in their book, *Lay My Burden Down*, write: "Psychologists have argued that long after emancipation and the legal end of segregation, the conflicts inherent in being black in America have led many black people to attempt to escape from the pressure of being second-class citizens through the use of drugs, alcohol and other forms of self-destructive behavior including suicide."

This notion is brought into sharp focus by the death of 19-year-old Cory Irvin, son of basketball great "Dr. J." Julius Irvin. Cory had resorted to drugs to solve personal problems. The drugs had not helped. Cory drove his car into a pond, killing himself. Police ruled that it could have been an accident. However, this is the kind of incident ruled "accident" to protect the family from the stigma of suicide.

CDC researchers state that one consequence of rising prosperity and social integration for African-Americans over the last few decades has been a distancing from family and church, leading to a sense of isolation during a crisis. The influence of gangs was not included.

Young African-Americans who buy into the myth of rugged individualism are unaware of the glass door that still exists for them. Those whom Dr. Aaron T. Beck describes in his book, *Prisoners of Hate*, encounter hostility and anger every day of their lives. Beck says, "Anger and hatred of human against human continues to take its toll today."

According to Poussaint, "Blacks had developed a crucial adaptive mechanism of mind-reading to judge other people's attitude and intentions towards them with some degree of accuracy, [but] racism can be benign and often difficult to recognize." Poussaint further notes, "persistent stress, racism and despair are the legacy of slavery.

Someone asked me, "What is this mind-reading?" I have the perfect example:

After completing an x-ray procedure at Good Samaritan Hospital in Los Angeles, I selected several items to purchase at the hospital's gift shop. I was standing behind another customer who was having something gift-wrapped when a third woman walked up.

I was acutely aware that she stood opposite me rather than behind me in line. I made eye contact with her. I knew she had a problem — immediately. She had that "back-of-the-bus" look in her eyes, the look of superiority and entitlement. She never asked to go ahead of me, so I was interested in seeing what would transpire.

"Who is next?" the cashier asked.

"I am," was my response and proceeded to give the cashier my purchases.

Without saying a word, the other woman slammed money on the counter and walked out in a huff.

"How rude!" the cashier said. Of course I agreed.

"Mind-reading" is the ability of one person to predict the behavior/action of another person before it happens.

All too often the black American youth encounters a "negative" mind-reading from others on a daily basis. One does not need to wonder about the untoward effect it has on self-esteem.

## Hispanic/Latino Americans

"Hispanic" is a term used by the Bureau of the Census to refer to "a person of Mexican, Puerto Rican, Cuban, Central or South American or other Spanish culture or origin, regardless of race," according to Gerald Mann and Barbara Mann in *Issues in Identifying Hispanics*. "Hispanic" and "Latino" are used interchangeably.

The 1990 census found that Hispanics represent nine percent of the total U.S. population. Over fifty percent of all Hispanics live in California and Texas. High birth rates and immigration have been cited as reasons for the rapid growth in this population. Hispanic girls now rank among the largest groups of girls in the country and are projected to remain high for many years to come.

Hispanics have similarities in terms of their cultural background, socioeconomic status, degree of acceptance in the dominant society, immigration experiences, color, and acculturation. Despite these similarities, Hispanics are heterogeneous, but they have fewer differences than those within other groups. Some cultural values, beliefs, and customs cut across different Hispanic groups.

### Family

The family is viewed as the single most important social unit in life. There is a strong sense of identification with and attachment to nuclear and extended families. The family structure is usually hierarchical and patriarchal, with special respect and much authority given to the husband and father. The oldest male is considered the head of the family, and everyone is expected to respect and obey his decisions. The cultural value of "machismo" identifies the Hispanic male as knowledgeable, fearless, and a good provider and protector of the family. Thus, sex-role identification for the Hispanic is somewhat different than that of the general population in the United States due to the machismo notion.

### Communication Style

Well-defined communication and interpersonal patterns exist within the family. Many Hispanics express opinions in an indirect, circular way. The use of hands and body language may be used to get a point across. Touching people while talking is acceptable. Hispanics prefer closeness to distance when interacting with others. Personal space is not as important as with non-Hispanics.

Spanish is the native language in over 50 percent of Hispanic homes.

## Individualism/Social Interaction

Hispanics are oriented towards persons rather than ideas, tasks, or abstractions. The need for smooth and pleasant social relationships is emphasized. Respect for authority figures such as teachers, physicians, and religious leaders is also stressed. Hispanics are also expected to show respect for the aged, the educated, and the wealthy.

## Religion

Catholicism is the predominant religion of sixty-eight percent of the Hispanic population. The remaining thirty-two percent are members of a variety of Christian, non-Catholic organizations. Among adolescents, males tend to become irregular in their religious practices.

## Materialism and Success

Prestige and respect are bestowed upon persons with property. The individual is taught the value of cooperation, mutual assistance, and sharing whenever necessary within the extended family. Currently, the entire family is responsible for the financial welfare of the family.

## Concept of Time

Time orientation is to the present with an eye towards the future. Punctuality is not demanded. Hispanics place greater value on the quality of interpersonal relationships than on the length of time in which they take place. Many Hispanics have adopted this nation's business standards and practices, which has altered their attitudes toward time in terms of punctuality.

As discussed in Chapter 2 on adolescent behavior, early adolescence is a critical time for all youths. The CDC Youth Risk Behavior Surveillance (1999) and other national surveys show that domestic problems are more prevalent among Hispanic girls than in white, Asian, or African-American girls.

One comprehensive survey, The Commonwealth Fund: The Latest Available Survey on the Health of Adolescent Girls (1997), found that the tendency to engage in risky behaviors differs significantly across racial and ethnic groups. In the study, non-Hispanic white and Hispanic girls were more likely to engage in risky behaviors than African-Americans or Asian-American girls. Hispanic and Asian girls exhibited more depressive symptoms than their African-American or non-Hispanic white peers. Hispanic-Americans described themselves as feeling moderately to severely negative about their own lives, followed closely by Asian-Americans, non-Hispanic whites, and lastly African-Americans.

Most disturbing of all, health risk data showed that Hispanic girls rank highest in rates of suicide. Alarmingly, Hispanic girls lead the nation in suicide. Most disturbing is the fact that one in three Hispanic girls reports seriously considering suicide — the highest rate of any racial or ethnic group. Hispanic girls are most likely to consider seriously, make a concrete plan for, and attempt suicide. The statistics point to a dire state of affairs. Among female high-school students in 1997, the suicide rate for Hispanic girls was one-and-a-half times that of their African-American and non-Hispanic white counterparts.

An even greater number of Hispanic girls that year had made a concrete plan to kill themselves. More specifically, of high school students, close to one-fourth of Hispanic girls had made a suicide plan, as compared to one-sixth of African-American females and one-fifth of non-Hispanic white girls.

Furthermore, serious consideration of suicide by Hispanic girls, an initial and triggering risk factor, has reached epidemic proportions. Close to one out of every three high school Hispanic girls had considered suicide, in comparison to one out of every five African-American girls and one in every four non-Hispanic white girls.

With the current statistics that Hispanic girls now rank as the largest group of girls in the country and are projected to remain so for the next fifty years, The National Coalition of Hispanic and Human Service Organizations, decided to address these issues. In 1998, the coalition launched a series of focus group meetings across the nation. The focus groups included girls ages nine to fourteen, their parents, and youth workers. This one-year endeavor resulted in a published report of the findings, The State of Hispanic Girls.

This report reinforced the national finding concerning risk behavior among Hispanic girls. Tragically, each focus group had at least one girl who had contemplated, attempted, or committed suicide. The most prevalent causative factors identified were the acculturation process, discrimination and racism, sexual and physical abuse, and family disruptions. Of these four, acculturation and family disruptions were more frequently precursors to suicide ideation.

Hispanic boys experience the same pressures as Hispanic girls: acculturation, racism, prejudice, discrimination, and family disruptions. However, suicide among Hispanic boys is not as high as among Hispanic girls. As the family system becomes less capable of satisfying the boys' psychological needs, Hispanic boys deal with their emotional pain, or psychache, by joining gangs. The gang becomes a "family surrogate," providing nourishment for the boys' emotional needs. They can cope with their psychache in ways sanctioned by the gang culture, either blunting it with alcohol or drugs, or acting out with violent behavior.

Alcohol, drugs, and violence are a potent part of gang dynamics. These behaviors are sanctioned in this male environment as "machismo." These boys experience a pervasive sense of helplessness and powerlessness in environments that are unpredictable, as in the family. Often they provoke violence to express their intense rage or commit symbolic suicide, becoming violent with the implicit intent of being killed. One youth worker refers to gangs as indulging in "group suicide."

In past studies, culture played a critical role in buffering Hispanic adolescents from risky behaviors and activities. At present, some of these cultural protections appear to be self-limited. First-generation immigrant youths report fewer risky behaviors than acculturated second or third-generation boys.

Current data reveal that increased acculturation to American Society leads to increased risky behavior and suicide among Hispanic girls. The process of acculturation is a major stressor to adolescent girls. As one youth worker from New York said, Hispanic adolescents here live in two worlds, one outside (at school) and one inside (at home.)"

A youth worker from California declared:

> In recent immigrant families, I find that culture is important and very much a part of the daily life of girls. Family values are still important. But these values are lost through time, especially traditional

values. Many immigrant parents feel that to succeed in [the] U.S. they must lose certain traditional values and acquire values of the American culture.

Focus group participants underscored the fact that challenges relating to family and culture, traditional gender role expectations, and acculturation are unique to Hispanic girls. According to the parents and youth workers, cultural adaptation poses special difficulties for these girls. For many girls of Hispanic origin, maintaining additional values in the contemporary American cultural context has become a real struggle.

One parent from New Mexico associated acculturation with loss of identity: "I don't seem to fit in either culture." Other parents stressed that Hispanic girls face additional pressures because they often have to serve as a bridge between two cultures for the sake of the family, a situation that gives them added responsibility at an early age, as expressed in the following statements.

> I see that our children have to interpret in many systems for the family... the child is the one that has to go before the system to talk about the family, make things happen for the family, and then the parents lose control of their children. (Youth Worker, New York).

The immigration experience itself may result in a range of predictable family conflicts. Immigrant children tend to acquire English-language skills and media knowledge of mainstream American culture at a much more rapid pace than their parents. This process causes a widening cultural gap within the family and results in marginalizing, developing a marginal ethnic identity. The marginalization divide affects girls more than boys.

In this process, religious ties and beliefs that assail suicide are minimized. One youth worker from California said that he had several cases where young girls have wanted to kill themselves:

"In most cases it's usually related to sexual abuse or molestation. . . no one was there for the girls when they need them. They couldn't deal with the emotional pain. Her only way out was to try to kill herself."

The youth worker also cited the case of a young Hispanic male:

"Jaime, age 14, entered the gang life at the age of 13 and later dropped out of school. His father abused alcohol, as well as the mother and Jaime, the oldest son. The mother told Jaime to understand, not to worry. 'He [his father] felt bad because he was unable to financially care for the family and send money to help his parents.' Jaime felt helpless and powerless to help the family, as a man. He joined a gang and began risk behaviors. He was found dead in his car from an apparent overdose; suicide was not ruled out. His sister expressed that Jaime started to withdraw from the family and listen to 'bad' music, and talked about leaving. He seemed to feel better for a time after he joined the gang".

Hispanic cultural values and practices exist in Hispanic culture, but among Hispanic adolescents, as among all adolescents, this stage of development is a critical time. Hispanic youths experience the same developmental, social, biological, and emotional changes. Among high-risk Hispanic adolescents, these changes supersede internalization of cultural values and practices. Parents, counselors, teachers, and peers should become familiar with

"Stormy Adolescence", presented in Chapter 2, and need to intervene when indicated.

The interaction of cultural, social and racial factors that impact adolescent suicide is very complex and needs more refined, as well as more culturally competent, persons such as teachers, counselors and health professionals. Those who are culturally different should not be criticized for being different, and the positive aspects of their culture should be stressed.

We need to keep in mind Hall's conclusion that it is impossible to communicate cultural understanding to anyone who has not lived through the experience. Tolerance of racial differences and of multicultures is needed in the United States among all of us.

One of the most enlightning findings is that today the adolescent most likely to commit suicide is the European American male and the American Indian, according to available sources. The plausible explanation is the emphasis on individual responsibility for a problem, an obsession with time and success, and an orientation towards the future or no orientation towards the future. When in the mind of the youth the future becomes the present, success is blocked, mental pain is present, the whole situation becomes hopeless, and suicide is imminent.

Native American youths lack the future orientation of European Americans. Their orientation is toward the present. There is no obsession with time, and sharing of responsibility is part of the culture. Poverty, frequent losses and discrimination are a present reality. Suicide becomes an escape to freedom. While there is plenty of time, circumstances in the present are likely to continue the feeling of imprisonment and entrapment described by Lafromboise and Bigfoot. According to Durkheim, suicide is an ultimate act of defiance with social origins. The deep wounds suffered by the Native Americans in incidents such as Wounded Knee and The Walk of Tears have been slow to heal.

Asian Americans have a lower suicide rate than both Native Americans and European Americans, although some Asian ethnic groups have a higher suicide rate than others. For example, the Japanese are more tolerant of suicide and experience a higher rate than the Chinese. Filipinos are mainly Catholic and, also, frown on suicide. Apparently, acculturation and being caught between cultures are problems more for foreign-born Asians than for those born in the United States.

African-Americans have experienced severe assimilation and acculturation problems due in part to the legal segregation of the races until less than half a century ago. Cultural differences and skin color continue to perpetuate the problem today. Psychologist Sandra Cox states, "upwardly mobile black youths who have bought into the myth of 'rugged individualism' are the ones who have the most difficulty." They have distanced themselves from family and the church. Support is lacking in stressful situations.

The concept of the glass door is a daily experience for most African-Americans, but many of the young "don't know how doors were opened in the first place," says Dorothy I. Height, of the Council of Negro Women. Some have not learned the protective device of mind-reading that Poussaint described to detect subtle racism and discrimination.

Although time is flexible, there is an orientation towards the future. Frustrated, feeling isolated and hopeless, a young African-American does not see the possibility of a successful outcome in the future. The future is now and so is the pain. Suicide is the youth's logical solution.

Hispanic Americans have a lower suicide rate than any of the other five major cultural groups. They are largely Catholic, and the church teaches suicide is a sin. However, a recent study found that while the suicide rate is lowest among Hispanic Americans, the rate of attempted suicide is higher than for any other group. The problems of acculturation exist, and youths very often feel caught between cultures, only marginally living in the American culture.

Finally, although culture cannot be taught as language can, more attention and information should be devoted to an appreciation of our rich cultural heritages in order to ease tensions and improve understanding.

Chapter Twelve

# The Juvenile Justice System

*We're blaming the children and focusing on all kinds of initiatives to lock them up, put them behind bars, kick them out of school.*

*The ones who are guilty — the ones who are the real perpetrators — are us.*

—Phillip Bracey
Massachusetts Social Worker

L urking within the trials and tribulations of adolescence is often a negative interaction with the juvenile justice system. Lacking experience and good judgment, some youths engage in behavior that is unacceptable to society, bringing them to the attention of law enforcement and sometimes resulting in incarceration or circumstances that can lead to suicide.

When teenagers engage in illegal behavior, we need to consider the reasons for such behavior. Dr. Joseph Teicher advises, "If a teenager causes trouble, look at the trouble two ways. One, it is a way of adapting or solving a problem even though it may not be a good way. And two, it is a signal for help. Misbehaving teenagers are rebels with a cause."

The reasons encounters with law enforcement can be negative are twofold. One, there is a lack of understanding and sensitivity toward adolescents. Two, the adolescent fears confrontation with the law and its unknown consequences. Therefore, the problem that youths experience are compounded rather than addressed. Feeling humiliated and caged, with no way out, many attempt suicide, some successfully.

Deon Whitfield and Durell Feaste who committed suicide last year were among the statistics along with countless others. The two had been under the supervision of the California Youth Authority. They were put in isolation for 23 hours per day. Isolation is a major risk factor for teenagers. The two hanged themselves in their cells.

Jason has a similar story:

Sixteen year-old Jason could only think about having his own car. All the boys at school seemed so "cool" when they drove cars, and having a car gave them independence. Jason wanted to be like them. He continually talked to his best friend, Tim, about wanting a car. He could not afford a car with what he earned from his part-time job at the market, nor could his grandmother afford to buy one for him; she could barely make ends meet. Jason lived with his grandmother, who was awarded sole custody when his unwed mother overdosed on drugs.

One sunny afternoon, on his way to work at the market, he spotted a convertible with the keys in the ignition. He found the opportunity to drive the car irresistible. He forgot about work, took the car, and went to pick up Tim. Finally, he felt free!

When he arrived at Tim's house, Tim said, "You shouldn't have stolen it!" Yet, the two went for a joy ride for several hours.

Later that evening when Jason came home, the police were waiting for him. As he was led away to juvenile hall, he looked at his grandmother and said, "I'm sorry." While at juvenile hall he attempted suicide.

Like most teenagers, Jason found total confinement difficult. The suicide attempt is a form of rebellion against the juvenile justice system, even though he had committed an offense.

The time Jason spent being detained was extremely difficult for him. He was transferred from juvenile hall to the Southern California Youth Correctional Reception Center and Clinic to be evaluated before being assigned to a long-term facility. He was there so long that it seemed as if administrators forgot to transfer him.

Each time his grandmother visited him at the Southern Youth Correctional Reception Center and Clinic, Jason would ask how long he was going to be incarcerated. His grandmother would tell him she did not know how long but that he was going to be transferred to another youth facility. Jason told her how hard it was being confined, with nothing interesting to do. He was bored. Boredom is intolerable punishment for teenagers.

One month passed. Then two months. Jason became more restless. He felt that officials had forgotten about him and that he was getting nowhere. He felt that his situation was hopeless.

One day, Jason was observed carving his grandmother's initials into his wrist with a nail file. He was seen by a psychiatrist, who felt that Jason was not in crisis. Based on this, the staff did not feel the need to watch Jason closely.

Several days later, as an act of frustration, he stopped up the toilet and flooded the unit where he lived with a group of boys. He was disciplined by being put in solitary isolation in a room with a video camera monitor. He was not put on suicide watch, nor was he monitored on the video camera. Instead, the staff concentrated their attention on another suicidal youth.

The following evening, during routine room checks, Jason was found hanging by a sheet attached to the metal frame of the video camera steel cable line.

In another incident similar to Jason's, the parents of 17-year-old Lam sued the county, charging negligence when Lam committed suicide after reportedly being told that he was going to be in jail for a long, long time. He had been told this, based on his trial records and the charges for which he had been booked. Lam had escaped twice before from juvenile hall, where he had been placed for stealing a car and falsely identifying himself as a policeman.

The family brought suit against the county because they contended that jail staff were cognizant of Lam being suicidal and failed to monitor him.

Mike Males, author of *The Scapegoat Generation,* says he is driven to correct "the clear injustice" perpetrated by officials on young people. Such an injustice was felt by 13-year-old Samuel, as well as his parents.

Samuel was taken to juvenile hall on suspicion of auto theft and driving without a license. He was assigned to a private room while awaiting transfer to a juvenile camp. Dressed in county-issued sweatshirt, pants, T-shirt, and sneakers, Samuel was found hanging from an air vent, his bed sheet tied around his neck. A detention service officer had found him on a routine check. Samuel had complained to his dad earlier that a security guard had been "pushing" him around and "didn't like kids."

Emile Durkheim, the world-renowned sociologist, stated that "suicide is the ultimate act of defiance." Samuel took control over the only thing he had left, his life. The security guard would not be able to taunt him any more, and he would not have to deal with a system he perceived as unfair. A more sensitive detention staff possibly could have saved Samuel's life.

Adolescents fear being confronted by authority, even when no crime has been committed. Two teenagers, both 15 years old, were running away with a 12-year-old girl. They stole a car and were leaving town when they were pulled over by a state trooper. The three had made a suicide pact to shoot themselves if stopped by law enforcement. The state trooper was able to get the gun before the girl could complete the suicide pact. The three died together. The two boys had gotten into trouble earlier in the week at their school in North Carolina.

Here, the trooper was only doing his job, but the incident illustrates the poor problem-solving skills of adolescents and their fear of police and of unknown consequences. Impulsivity is a factor in adolescent suicide.

Another senseless tragedy that was triggered by a brush with the law involved two young people who just wanted to be together.

Danielle, 14 years old, was a good student, but quiet and a bit moody. She had met Lawrence, 17, several months earlier. Danielle's parents objected to their relationship, but she seemed obsessed with Lawrence. She ran away from home four times to be with him. After her parents reported her as a runaway, Danielle was located in an unoccupied private home with Lawrence.

Before police could take them from the house, the modern-day Romeo and Juliet each took a single gunshot, the result of an apparent suicide pact. The officers found them one on top of the other, clad in T-shirts and shorts. They were determined to be together and were going to override their parents.

In the next example, the pain of a broken relationship, as well as problems at school, added to the reaction of having a brush with the law.

It was 6 A.M. when the police spotted 17-year-old Matthew driving the Toyota his parents had reported missing. They had reported their gun missing as well. A chase ensued. The chase ended in front of his girlfriend's house. Matthew fired twice, striking himself in the head. He had broken up with his girlfriend. The chase by police of the emotionally distraught adolescent apparently pushed him over the edge.

In another example, Regan, who had been accused of several crimes, felt the prospect of serving jail time was too much for him.

Seventeen-year-old Regan was a loner, but bright, with an interest in baseball. His school attendance problems had prompted his transfer from Palos Verdes High School to a continuation school. However, other than occasionally ditching school, he had not had any problems. He was about to enroll in a junior college in Mississippi, after earning his high school equivalency certificate. His parents were divorced, and his father lived in Mississippi.

Then he was accused of being a suspect in two robberies and tying up a woman during the commission of one robbery. Regan was overwhelmed. He died of a self-inflicted gunshot wound.

Consequently, a juvenile justice system that demonstrates sensitivity can lead to positive outcomes for our youth.

On a cold but sunny morning, during all the pomp and circumstance of a formal graduation, Angel, an 18-year-old, presented his speech. He had been one of the best students in his high school class and was preparing to attend city college as a business major.

Before he spoke, Angel's eyes moved back and forth across each row of the audience, looking for his father in the crowd of faces. His father collected bottles and cans for money and had used that money to buy Angel a new suit for graduation. Angel wanted him to be proud. There in the middle aisle towards the rear sat his father, waving and smiling. He appeared as proud as Angel wanted him to be.

Angel graduated with about a thousand other students — all graduates from the juvenile justice system. He and his peers had "messed up" along the way and landed in a juvenile detention camp.

Angel had excelled in his classes until he reached junior high school. He did not like his home life and became involved in a gang over his father's objections. After getting involved with the gang, Angel's grades dropped, and he was absent from school a great deal. He was arrested at age 14 and, eventually, ended up in the juvenile camp.

At the camp, two probation officers took an interest in Angel. The two used their own money to pay for him to take the SAT college entrance examination. They used their day off to escort him to the test. Angel scored 1090 on the SAT. Angel was fortunate to have two probation officers who believed in him. On his graduation day, Angel showed them, and his father, that all he needed was someone to believe in him.

For numerous reasons, teenagers are having brushes with law enforcement at an increasing rate. The incidence is unlikely to decline in the near future, as many believe that it is tougher to be a teenager today than in any other time in history.

Many of them are not "bad" kids, just immature and impulsive. In other words, they are simply young people who use poor judgment. Sometimes poorly trained police and juvenile detention staff, in an effort to "teach the kid a lesson," make a poor situation worse. Dehumanized and confined, a teenager may react defiantly by taking his or her own life. It is a choice no child should have to make.

Chapter Thirteen

# Music As An Influence

*... Suicide is a theme found in most genres of music; few have to be defended against allegations of actually causing suicide.*

—Suicide Information & Education Centre

A precise cause-and-effect relationship between genres of music and teenage suicide has not been determined, but anecdotal evidence suggests that there may be some influence from certain kinds of music. At the very least, the presence of music that emphasizes alienation and despair in the lifestyle of a young person could help alert friends and family to other co-existing tendencies toward suicide.

The purpose of this chapter is to examine the issue of suicide and music in vulnerable teenagers. Five teen suicides associated with music — Michael, Terry, John, Walter and Harold — will be discussed, along with a closer look at heavy metal music and research on the genre.

## Michael

"Pop, I believe old Oz has the solution," sixteen-year-old Michael told his father. They were talking about a driving-under-the-influence (DUI) arrest Michael had received four weeks earlier. His father reassured Michael that they could work things out with the violation.

Later, Michael attended a beer party at the home of a friend whose parents were away and out of town. He spent the evening driving around town and drinking beer, then listening to heavy metal music behind the house with some of the other beer party friends. According to the police and Michael's father, Ozzy Osbourne's "Blizzard of Oz" was the last tape Michael listened to before returning to the party. Ozzy Osbourne is the British heavy metal rock star.

In the early hours of the morning, Michael entered the kitchen and asked his friends to take a seat on the couch facing him. After writing a suicide note, he picked up a handgun, leaned back on a kitchen stool, and blew a hole through the refrigerator door. He raised the pistol to his right temple and pulled the trigger. He died instantly.

Michael's father stated that the teenager had been frustrated and depressed about the DUI violation, but he hadn't picked up on the reference to "Oz."

"It wasn't until after the shooting [that] I found the cassette in his tape deck and I understood what the young'un was talking about," Michael's father said. The song was about suicide.

## Terry

Eighteen-year-old Terry played hockey one evening. His friends noticed nothing unusual about the quiet, moody youth who had recently been chosen to be the goalie in an upcoming tournament. He told them he was going to the edge of the sea with his grandfather the following morning, to hunt polar bears. No one knew if this was a normal activity for Terry.

Unnoticed, Terry left the hockey game, went home, and turned up the rock music on his stereo. Then he hanged himself in his room with a telephone cord. No suicide note was found.

"There was no warning," one friend, who dug the grave, said. "Everybody feels a little bit guilty, as if they should have seen this coming. Was there something someone should have done?"

## John

In a different twist, parents of nineteen-year-old John filed suit against Ozzy Osbourne, the British heavy metal rock star, after their son shot himself to death with a .22-caliber gun as he listened to a tape of Osbourne's song, "Suicide Solution." He was still wearing stereo headphones when his body was discovered.

The lyrics in "Suicide Solution" are part of what John's parents claimed spurred the teenager's suicide: *Breaking laws, knocking doors, but there's no one at home. Made your bed, rest your head, but you lie there and moan. Where to hide, suicide is the only way out. . .*

The suit claimed that the lyrics are satanic.

Osbourne's attorney contended that the song, "Suicide Solution," was actually anti-suicide and had been written about Osbourne's alcoholic friend, a singer named Bon Scott, who drank himself to death. The song was a response to the dangers of alcohol. The lawsuit was unsuccessful.

Osbourne is not the only rock star singled out as encouraging suicidal behavior. The British band Judas Priest was sued by families of eighteen-year-old Raymond and twenty-year-old Vance, who shot themselves two days before Christmas. The parents claimed that subliminal suicide messages on Priest's album "Stained Class" drove them to the act.

The judge on the case, Jerry Carr Whitehead, ruled that the subliminal messages that did exist on the album were not intentional, but "a chance combination of sounds," and did not prompt the suicide pact.

## Harold

Harold, a seventeen-year-old high school dropout, had a history of drug and alcohol abuse, but appeared to be on the road to recovery. Although he still used pot and alcohol, Harold had found a steady job as a cabinetmaker and appeared to be stable and satisfied, according to his mother.

Then, early one morning, Harold wrote a suicide note to his sister, borrowed a car, took a gun from the trailer of a friend with whom he had been boarding, and stopped by to visit his mother.

Harold told his mother that he had just returned from an adjacent city, where a girl he liked rejected his advances. His mother said Harold was visibly upset. He told her that he was going to visit his sister. Before he left his mother's house, Harold told her: "Mom, you will never see me again."

Near noon the same day, Harold's car was found by a stranger in the driveway of a home in another town. Draped across the front seat with a pistol in his hand and a bullet hole in his temple, Harold was still alive. A cassette of Osbourne's album, "Tribute," was in the tape deck.

## Walter

Seventeen-year-old Walter committed suicide while carrying an Ozzy Osbourne tape with the song, "Suicide Solution." Rabbi Arian, staff director of the Task Force on Youth Suicide for the Union of American Hebrew Congregations, asked the record industry to "voluntarily withhold release of songs whose lyrics advocate suicide."

Rabbi Arian further advised, "Record companies need to know that impressionable teens may take seriously the messages their artists convey. There's reason to believe that limiting the exposure of teenagers to ... rock music that actually advocates suicide might help reduce the suicide rate."

Arian explained, "When a kid is depressed and suicidal, certain environmental factors can serve as precipitants. There is a fairly substantial body of anecdotal evidence in the press of youths who've committed suicide after listening to rock music advocating suicide."

Adolescent suicide victims who are already in a vulnerable state of mind are susceptible to being influenced by the lyrics in a song — although they may be taken out of context or misinterpreted, as the lyrics in Ozzy Osbourne's "Suicide Solution." Anecdotal evidence suggests a direct link between listening to heavy metal music and adolescent suicide, according to the Suicide Information and Education Centre:

Heavy Metal Music and Suicide
Heavy metal is a subgenre of rock that has grown in popularity, especially among younger males. Metal bands

usually include a heavy bass guitar and extreme volume. The theme of metal is chaos, on an individual or societal level, and is what most clearly distinguishes metal from mainstream rock. Heavy metal carries on traditional countercultural concerns with social problems, but it departs from earlier rock music in that it does not offer hope, or solutions, for solving such problems.

It has been alleged that heavy metal lyrics, with themes of alienation and despair, have acted as precipitants to suicide among vulnerable adolescents.

Lester and Whipple point out that many young people who listen to heavy metal also listen to other types of music. These may also have lyrics concerning suicide, despair or isolation. It would thus be difficult to pinpoint a specific genre as being the direct and sole cause of suicide.

Other Research Data on Adolescents, Heavy Metal Music and Suicide

A simple cause-effect relationship does not exist between exposure to rock music and suicide.

Heavy metal music more often seems to become a problem for adolescents who are already disturbed and struggling with feelings of alienation. These adolescents may also lack positive role models, come into repeated conflict with authorities, abuse alcohol and drugs; and have a family of history violence and/or suicide.

Far from placing adolescents at risk of suicide, heavy metal music may have protective functions for some:

54% of a sample of male heavy metal fans who were interviewed said that their music served a purgative function, that is it helped to relieve feelings of anger. The music mirrored the emotional volatility brought on by the usual crises and conflicts of adolescence.

Rock lyrics, including those said to advocate destructive acts, may in some cases provide a medium for dealing with issues of death and for managing the anxieties these issues create.

A recent *Los Angeles Times* column by Dr. Joyce Brothers, a psychologist, responded to the mother of a fourteen-year-old boy who was disturbed by the suicide of another youth at school. In her response to the mother, Dr. Brothers wrote:

Adolescents today face a world in which the competition is intense and the opportunities are not as unlimited as they might appear to be. Education is vital for success in almost any field, and youngsters who are having trouble keeping up might feel threatened, especially if their parents have unrealistically high expectations. Listen to the lyrics of their music, and you might get a sense of the hopelessness, anger and depression that many young people feel. [*Los Angeles Times*, November 20, 2001]

I could not agree more!

Chapter Fourteen

# Death Wish: When Crossing Over Seems Better

*He was death-happy... not sad but more like 'The other side is gonna be so much more fun.' More like 'I can't wait to die.'*

—Friend of Chris Miller

The concept of a death wish does not appear in clinical or academic literature on suicidal behavior. The reason for this omission is not clear, but it is probably due to the fact that suicidal people talk about suicide in such a casual manner that they are not taken seriously. Therefore, they are not hospitalized, nor do they get the attention of mental health professionals.

As stated in Chapter Four, "Focus on the Family and the Village," it must be emphasized that the vast majority of suicides do not occur in mental health facilities, but in homes and communities. Perhaps academia and practicing mental health professionals have not yet specifically identified those who commit suicide as the result of a death wish.

Teenagers with a death wish have no discernible reason for wanting to commit suicide. They simply believe that conditions are going to be happier wherever it is people go when they leave the earth.

The origin and age of onset of a death wish are not known, but it can appear in childhood and can last over a period of years. Each negative experience or challenge is further proof that this life is not for them. One plausible explanation is chronic childhood depression or lack of optimism. Individuals with such problems are passive. They do not shape their world and their life; they are not proactive.

The idea of a death wish was first called to my attention by an extensive article on the topic in *Vanity Fair*. The article was given to me by my writing professor, who knew of my interest in adolescent suicide. Since that time, several cases in the news media have caught my attention. In addition, while I was discussing my interests with a young veterinary extern, Tija, she said, "My friend committed suicide. He had a death wish, but he didn't really think he was going to die." The same phenomenon is reported over and over again.

Several case examples of death wishes follow. The first concerns Chris, who had had a dark side since childhood. Chris convinced his girlfriend, Heidi, that life would be better on the other side.

In the darkness of the wee hours of a Sunday morning, two teenagers in love, Chris, 16, and Heidi, 15, parked her car along a scenic cliff at the edge of Rancho Palos Verdes, a rustic area of expensive homes, hiking paths, and dirt-bike trails. They hiked down a rugged path and ducked through a hole in a chain-link fence to get to the narrow, 100-foot-long concrete spillway locally known as "the diving board," and leaped 150 feet to the rolling surf below in order to end their lives.

"He seemed like a well-adjusted kid," Chris's grandfather said. "Just got his first job. Just got his first paycheck. I don't think his parents had any idea."

The prior fall, Chris had transferred from a local parochial school to San Pedro High School, where he quickly made friends. Both students and teachers could only remark how nice he seemed. He was college bound, and his grades were above average, As and Bs.

The "nice" Chris was apparently also complicated. He played guitar in a punk garage band. Behind his jocular façade, he had bouts with depression. Chris had wept over the suicide of Kurt Cobain, the angst-ridden grunge singer. He chose suicide as his topic in his creative writing class.

On the Friday before the incident, according to his friend Harvey, "Chris was really happy. He was going to help produce the fashion show that weekend. He's the last person you'd expect to do this."

Yet Mike, 16, who played in the garage band, Crump's Brother, with Chris, saw another side of him. Mike had been friends with Chris since childhood. Mike said, "I could always tell when Chris' dark side was holding sway by the makeup that he would periodically smear across his eyes.

"He talked about how he got depressed, but I never thought he would go this far." Mike stated that he did not know the source of Chris' depression, and he never asked.

In the car Chris had driven to the lover's leap, he had left a note written hastily on a brown paper bag, which read in part, "You can't fire me, I quit." The line had been taken from Kurt Cobain's song, "Scentless Apprentice" on Nirvana's "In Utero" album.

Heidi, a daughter of a wealthy family from the Palos Verdes Peninsula and Chris' girlfriend, had told her friends that she and her mother were fighting about Chris. The mother had forbidden Heidi to entertain Chris at home without a parent present. On Saturday the cleaning lady had reported that Heidi was home alone with Chris. The mother had grounded Heidi for three weeks, which upset Heidi.

Heidi's diary described her two lives. On the surface she wore a jovial mask, but inside she was gripped by hopelessness. Heidi left a note for her mother saying, "Too bad you believed Maria and not me. I don't want to be grounded anymore."

She was quoted as saying, "I will fly with the heavenly Father and my grandpa." She and her grandfather had a close relationship, but she left no words of affection for her parents. Heidi's mother said she had failed to see the warning signs, if any were present.

Perhaps the best-known case of death-wish suicide involved two best friends, Joe and Jeff, both 16 years old. The two hung out together all the time, getting high and cruising the streets of Fillmore, California. The incident is fully covered by Joe Morgenstern in "The Death-Wish Kids" in the October 1984 issues of *Vanity Fair*.

Joe had been born in Santa Paula, California and grew up in nearby Fillmore, a town of citrus and avocado groves. Joe had two older brothers, Darren and Derek, who adored him. His parents constantly argued.

Joe had retreated and become a dreamer. His parents had separated when Joe was in the fourth grade. Within a short time, Joe was in trouble at school, picking fights and talking back to his teacher. In the sixth grade, Joe made friends with Jeff. He needed a buddy, and Jeff had the sunny disposition he craved, as well as an eagerness to please. Jeff looked up to Joe.

Three years after Joe's mother and father separated, they were divorced. Joe's mother remarried and moved away from the home, just as his father had done. When the mother left, the father returned to the family bungalow, but Joe's life became unglued over the eight months after his mother had remarried. Joe hated his life at home. His father criticized him at every turn, saying that Joe's mother had indulged him for so long that he was unmanageable.

Soon after Jeff met Joe, Jeff's father became involved in an affair. Jeff's parents separated, but later reconciled. However, they continued to live on the brink of separation. Jeff's brother, Danny, apparently weathered this upheaval fairly well, while Jeff found refuge with Joe.

At the age of 12, in the seventh grade, Joe started drinking and doing drugs. He smoked marijuana before school, and at lunchtime he went home to an empty house.

Jeff's behavior at home began to resemble Joe's. He, too, was becoming withdrawn. Jeff's parents became concerned. They attempted to separate the boys, but Jeff needed Joe. The two had become close friends, so close that people in Fillmore referred to them by a single name, as Jeff-and-Joe.

Jeff and Joe had some good times together, but mostly they were preoccupied with their troubles, including their fights with their fathers and their shared conviction that Fillmore was a prison where nothing would ever change for the better. Both felt that life had only unhappiness to offer.

Soon, and for the first time, the boys considered suicide. The boys fantasized that they would go to Pole Creek, where Jeff liked to fish, swallow some pills and simply lie down on the grass to die. It was only a passing thought, a matter of "yeah, yeah, someday . ."

Joe's relationship with his father went from bad to worse after the father moved his girlfriend and her son into the house. Joe saw no future for himself. He concluded that he would never get out of Fillmore.

Joe and Jeff discussed suicide for a second time, and this time they considered the best way of going about it. They had no firm plans to kill themselves tomorrow, next week, or even next month, but they did decide that jumping off the cliff would be practical and painless.

Jeff and Joe continued to hang out together, drinking, driving, and talking. One day Joe blurted out to a female classmate that they planned to fly through the air off a cliff. He also told her they would come back alive.

At one point, Joe turned to Jeff and said, "Let's go kill ourselves."

"Yeah, Jeff replied, "Let's go."

That was all it took: The two proceeded to drive off a cliff in a suicide attempt. Jeff died; Joe survived.

Teenagers who have a death wish seem to have a notion of "coming back." They appear to be reassured that their current situation will be improved if they commit suicide. When the action will be taken is usually left vague. No real need to rush is felt, and the triggering incident is difficult to identify. This fantasy aspect of adolescent suicide is not identified in current clinical and academic psychological literature. It merits further study.

Chapter Fifteen

# Guilt As A Problem In Grieving

*You feel a profound sense of failure that you could not prevent his death. Closely tied to your sense of failure is the implied rebuke: You could not offer him enough... of whatever he needed so that he would want to live. You feel a terribly personal abandonment, that he preferred to die rather than be alive with you.*

—Barbara D. Rosof

## The Worst Loss

It is estimated that at least six people are affected by every suicide, with the mother being the most profoundly affected by the death of a child. Although death can be a devastating event for the entire family, each of us experiences the loss of a loved one differently.

During a class discussion on suicide at UCLA, a young woman in her mid-thirties began to cry as she spoke of a neighbor girl who had shot herself some 20 years prior in Seattle. She gave me the phone number of the girl's mother, suggesting that I call her for the details surrounding her daughter's suicide.

Initially, the mother volunteered to provide whatever information she could. She recalled what a surprise and how traumatic her daughter's suicide had been, not only for her family, but for the entire community as well. One sibling dropped out of school; others also attempted suicide. However, as the mother began recalling the relevant events, she became overwhelmed and insisted that the suicide evoked too many painful memories. Other than the fact that the girl was 19 and shot herself to death, the source of the girl's pain is unknown to me.

Interestingly, it was a student, Anne, who inspired the research for this chapter. "What you should be doing is writing about the guilt a family feels after a suicide," she told me. Anne's brother had committed suicide at the age of 17. He got involved with the wrong crowd and with drugs. Failing grades in school led to his dropping out and, eventually, committing suicide. The family suffered collective guilt as well as individual regret for not having intervened.

One's world can be shattered by a telephone call or a knock on the door, by a friend or policeman. Our young person has chosen to take his or her own life. We feel numb. We are in shock and disbelief. How can this be? How could I not see it coming? Why? These are some of the questions we ask ourselves over and over again. Death by suicide is the most difficult to resolve because of its unexpectedness. However, as previously stated, it is not always unexpected.

# Grief and Mourning

Grief and mourning are universal experiences. Grief refers to a subjective feeling and mood caused by the loss. Mourning refers to the processes by which grief is resolved. A loss through suicide is a major crisis; everyone touched by the loss may react differently. Some may grieve immediately, while others, in shock or numb, will have delayed pain. Although not all survivors will exhibit a particular pattern of grieving in exactly the same order, there are five phases that are generally observed. These phases were originally described by Dr. Elizabeth Kubler-Ross in her widely read book, *On Death and Dying*, in which she identified five phases of dying, not grieving. Since then, the five phases have become distinguished as stages of grief as well. Other grief therapists have described the path of the grief process, some using different terms, but basically the process remains the same:

Shock and disbelief

Anger

Bargaining

Depression

Acceptance

It is important to emphasize that no time line be imposed on any phase, as an individual may go back and forth until final acceptance occurs. Even then, some incident may trigger an emotional response or backsliding.

## Shock and Disbelief

Numbness, emptiness, and denial are the first responses to the suicide. Denial is a common reaction to any death. The survivor cannot accept the devastating loss that has occurred. "Denial is a mental defense mechanism which not only enables the survivor to absorb the traumatizing news, but also acts as a buffer to allow the person to acknowledge the reality of death slowly," states Elizabeth M. Varcarolis in *Foundations of Psychiatric Mental Health Nursing.*

Anita, a nurse and mother of 22-year-old Kurt Brian, wrote, "When the police officer came to our door to inform us of Kurt Brian's death, he explained that Kurt Brian would not be recognizable as it most likely had been five months. 'That doesn't mean he's dead?' Later, I remembered saying that. I thought how stupid I was, not realizing... It was such a shock. could not fathom [his being dead]."

Denial can be so strong in intensity that one simply refuses to believe. When a 21-year-old boy was killed in Chattanooga, Tennessee, his mother reflected, "At first I was in total disbelief. My son died early Sunday morning, and we didn't see him until Monday afternoon. I went to the funeral home knowing I was going to see someone else. I could not believe this had happened."

Survivors may accept the death but deny that death was self-inflicted. They also may function in a mechanical way to get through the funeral. Discussions of the pain, also, may be avoided. The protective mechanism of denial may be present for a few days or several months. Gentle and consistent emotional support encourages an atmosphere that will enable the person in denial to arrive at his or her own level of adjustment, according to William J. Kirk in *Adolescent Suicide.*

## Anger

Most often, the initial stage of shock and disbelief is followed by anger, particularly when painful feelings begin to surface. The survivor's anger may be directed towards the school, the victim, himself or herself, or God. Statements such as "He should not have jilted her. It's his fault" or "Why did God let this happen to him? He was a good son" are common.

To some degree, anger should be expected. Allowing its expression is healthy and needs to be encouraged in an appropriate context, Kirk believes. As time passes, anger should be directed towards the act of suicide, not at others.

## Bargaining

Through bargaining, the individual negotiates with God in an attempt to reverse or postpone the death. One mother stated, "Bargaining can occur with sudden death. I did it. I went into her room and kept touching her things and bargaining to see her one more time. I negotiated with God. I promised to go to church... it was important this time to keep my part of the bargain, so I promised to be a more active parent, a more caring neighbor, a more supportive friend, a better person in every way. Maybe that would bring my daughter back!"

During the bargaining phases, as listed, promises are made to alter life styles, go to church more often, give to church, love thy neighbor, do whatever one thinks God wants to hear. The promise is made in exchange for the return to life of the person who committed suicide.

## Depression

Depression is a common response to loss and is a difficult phase of grieving. Feelings of sadness, hopelessness, or helplessness may occur immediately or several weeks following the suicide. Depression may last for any number of months, depending on the closeness of the survivor to the victim, i.e., parent, relative, or friend, and the status of the relationship, i.e., healthy, marginal, or conflicted, according to Kirk. Unfinished business with the victim determines to some extent the length of the depression.

Professional help may be needed to overcome the depression if it becomes severe or chronic. Otherwise, encouraging a return to normal functioning is recommended. Participation in a grief and loss support group has been a great benefit to many, especially survivors of suicide, who may not receive the same social support as other mourners. Survivors tend to be avoided and even blamed for the suicide, as reflected in the statement "They should be ashamed of themselves for letting him commit suicide."

## Acceptance

Resolution is an adaptive phase of mourning. "Acceptance indicates a more complete awareness of the extent of the loss and an ability to function without the deceased," states Kirk. He adds, "The survivors show a willingness to discuss the loss more openly and with less pain and discomfort. Mourners who integrate a healthy acceptance of the loss have generally redefined their relationship with the deceased. That redefinition incorporates a willingness to move forward with their own lives without guilt or burden."

## Grief Work

Grief work is a task that must be done by the individual. As stated earlier, the phases of grief may not be distinct from each other and may overlap. In addition, other emotions, such as fear and guilt, may appear during the grief process. Fear refers to feeling alone, vulnerable to the world as an unsafe place, and fearful that someone else, also, may be lost.

Suicide differs from other forms of death because it almost always produces overwhelming guilt. Guilt is absent when the grieving parent, relative, or friend feels no responsibility for the suicide. In the case of the parents' guilt, they may have made recognizable mistakes in parenting for which they rightfully feel guilty.

One thing one must learn is that suicide is never a singular event. Many things go into the adolescent's decision to end his or her own life; pain, confusion, hopelessness and helplessness, perfectionism, and poor self-esteem may all play a role. However, we frequently forget that whatever our failures — as parents, siblings, children, or friends — these failures alone were not enough to make our loved one take his or her life.

The survivor of a suicide reproaches himself or herself for real or fancied acts of negligence or omissions in relationships with the deceased. Edward Dunne and Merryl Maleska Wilbur, in *Survivors of Suicide*, describe reactions of suicide survivers:

> The survivors of most deaths experience some sense of guilt. This comes from a feeling that it is somehow unfair that we are still alive while our loved one has suffered and died. Additionally, it is rare not to feel that we could have done more or been nicer to the deceased. Sometimes fleeting, sometimes quite intense, guilt is almost always a part of the picture when death occurs. For survivors of suicide, the intensity of guilt feelings is often greatly out of proportion to our contribution to

the event. Some of us remember this self-blaming as a way of not feeling helpless.

Barbara Rosof, in *The Worst Loss*, lists three unique problems associated with suicide loss and guilt. First are the parents' feelings of the worst failure. Second is a sense of personal rejection, and third is the stigma attached to suicide.

Failure to take action induced guilt in Anne's family after her brother's suicide. Although undeserved, the sense of failure and unworthiness for Anne's family was pervasive and prolonged.

Personal rejection, experienced by a family, is a feeling of not being wanted by the suicide victim, not being good enough to continue life for, abandonment, a slap in the face, devalued, or incomplete. The feelings of worthlessness, incompetence, and inadequacy are universal, according to Rosof.

Anita, the mother of Kurt Brian, said, "I agree that the feelings of guilt are the most prominent in suicide bereavement. I did not have family support after Brian's death. My sisters, both out of state, never called or wrote. My mother was local, but blamed us for his death." I used to be afraid I would forget what he looked like, the sound of his voice. Now it is almost 19 years since we have seen our son. I know now I could never forget."

Suicide-related guilt may take various forms. One factor complicating the understanding of guilt is the definition of suicide because suicide is viewed differently in different cultural settings and in different ethnic, age, and other groups. Suicide-related guilt may be culturally rooted and is not necessarily the same as shame. The Christian attitude toward suicide is commonly presented as a reaction to, as well as a departure from, the permissive attitudes toward suicide practices that prevailed in the Greco-Roman world.

Full growth of the moral sense is not merely a conditioning of childhood. Moral sense is developed by actual life experience — through circumstances and human relations — a view much more tolerant to the kind of guilt experiences in reaction to the suicide of close ones.

Guilt is accompanied by a number of other feelings. It may involve a sense of sin or fear of punishment by others. It involves a weakness and inferiority. Some believe that guilt is a form of anxiety in which an individual anticipates punishment. That individual believes that he or she has "sinned" and fears that God will attack and punish him or her.

Rosof states that the best way to deal with this situation is to make a statement such as "Abbe died last week. He took his own life." Rosof advises that one's willingness to speak of this painful event relieves the other person, giving him or her permission to speak as well, having a "model for direction."

Just as a suicide can sharply affect individuals, it can likewise fall heavily on the familial relationships that include brothers, sisters, parents, friends, uncles, aunts, and cousins. Some families can be blown apart by the guilt and blame that can follow a suicide. Some may be drawn together, supporting one another in their collective grief and confusion. Other families go on in silence and pretend that nothing has happened or that the suicide was an accidental death.

The self-recriminations and guilt, however, often may be poorly founded, and the real causes to be found elsewhere. In any case, the suicide of a child may lead to blame and guilt that tears at the marital bonds. Some parents are supportive of each other,' some retreat to endure the pain of their loss in silence. Divorce is common among couples with a child suicide.

Allison was 16 when Brenda, her 20-year-old sister, took an overdose of pills while she was away at college. The incident occurred 12 years ago, and everything changed radically. Her parents were caught up in Brenda's death and seemed to forget that Allison was alive. Allison began to wonder, "Maybe I'd get more attention if I were dead."

## Coping with Suicide

Coping with suicide is a multi-dimensional topic, with many approaches available. It has been noted that guilt in the right measure may help balance behavior, but when it becomes an interfering overriding force, it must be managed. Setting one's own standards, instead of trying to live up to the expectations of others, can offer freedom from heavy guilt.

Social support and professional counseling are standard recommendations for helping individuals cope with the suicide of a close loved one. Reaching out in some manner is a good way for relatives, friends, or neighbors to let the grief-stricken person know that they care and can be counted on for support. They may offer to go with him or her to a support group, or they may volunteer to baby-sit, shop, or run errands.

Compassion and understanding are crucial. Asking "How are you doing?" is helpful. However, one should not offer any of these dismissive clichés: "I know how you feel." "Why?" "At least he/she is out of pain." "It's time to get over it." "You've been hurting long enough."

One type of support group is Loving Outreach to Survivors of Suicide (LOSS) sponsored by Catholic Charities in the Chicago area. "We make sure everyone introduces themselves and explains why they're at the meeting," a LOSS representative explained. "No one is required to speak after that, but neither do we allow anyone to dominate the session. There's no agenda; people just speak from their own experiences and feelings. Since we all know first-hand what they're talking about, we can make very good listeners, and sharing — realizing that the anguish you're going through is normal — lightens the burden."

According to Rosof, parents who have lost a child through suicide have found the following helpful:

Prompt involvement of caregivers

Talking about what happened

Encouraging all family members to talk openly

Examining their guilt and re-appraising their own responsibility

Reaching out to others, marking anniversaries

Respecting the individual's own timetable for healing.

The sense of guilt can be crushing and can last for a lifetime. The suicide survivor gets caught up in the "if only" syndrome. Talking with a sympathetic advisor or friend may help one to arrive at a more objective outlook. Feelings of guilt are not necessary. An important step is to forgive oneself.

Chapter Sixteen

# Prevention Strategies

*I did not want to die, but I did not want to live as life existed.*

—Nancy
Suicide survivor

Evidence based on suicide survivors' accounts supports the assumption that the suicidal teenager is ambivalent about death. If their problems could be removed, then they would desire to live. They desire to die because the pain is intolerable. The immediate task at hand is not to resolve the precipitating problem, the triggering circumstance, but to prevent the suicide. Dr. Edwin Shneidman, the renowned suicidologist, states that the two most important questions to ask an adolescent threatening suicide are: "Where do you hurt?" and "How can I help?" One should not ask "why" suicide was chosen as a solution to the problem.

**Imminent Suicide Prevention Strategies:**

• Reduce the unbearable pain.

Feelings are important. Talk therapy helps. If the teen fails to talk to you, keep talking to him or her. Do not discount the way he/she feels: "Oh, don't feel that way."

- Fill the frustrated needs.

  Confront the "bully," discuss the rejection, provide social contact, etc.

- Provide a viable answer.

  "Other teenagers sometimes have the same problem(s) you're having. You may need a little help."

- Indicate alternatives.

  "There are several ways of dealing with the problem. One...Two..."

- Give transfusions of hope.

  "Tomorrow you may feel altogether differently. Give yourself some time."

- Play for time.

  Suggest a physical activity in the open fresh air such as walking, playing basketball, etc.

  Do not leave an actively suicidal person alone.

  Exercise often improves one's mood of depression.

- Increase the options.

  "We can go for a ride later, or to the movies if you like." A change in one's immediate environment can be helpful.

- Listen to the cry; involve others.

  "I sense the pain you're feeling. Perhaps we should

let someone help us who's had more experience with this than I've had. I believe Dr. Quinton James has a lot of experi-ence in this area (example only).

- Block the exit or escape from distress.

  "I need to make a contract with you that you will not hurt yourself while we work this out."
- Involve previous positive patterns of successful coping.

  Help individual recall good previous problem-solving skills.

## Primary Suicide Prevention Strategies:

- Promote a healthy identity and self-esteem during the formative years, long before adolescence.
- Parents, schools, places of worship, and social welfare share the responsibility of promoting a healthy self-concept in children.
- Teaching healthy coping strategies and keeping lines of communication open.
- Avoid circumstances that have shown to "trigger" suicidal behavior in teens, i.e., social isolation, a new high school, trivorce, humiliation, substance abuse, poor parental relationships, rejection, judicial system ignorance, the "contagion" effect and problem music.

## Secondary Suicide Prevention Strategies:

- Discuss suicidal behavior when other health issues are discussed.

- Community mental health professionals help parents identify teens at risk.
- October is one month to be especially aware of suicidal behavior in older teenagers.
- Peer support programs have been found to be effective.
- Gatekeeper programs that are on the alert for neighborhood teenagers with serious problems.

**Tertiary Suicide Prevention Strategies:**

- Rehabilitate the adolescent after a suicide attempt.
- Teach parents early warning signs of trouble and make referrals to support groups and agencies. Working together, we can prevent suicide in vulnerable adolescents.

Appendix A

# Risk Factors For Youth Suicide

## Biopsychosocial Risk Factors

- Hopelessness
- Impulsive and/or aggressive tendencies
- History of trauma or abuse
- Previous suicide attempt
- Family history of suicide
- Alcohol and other substance use disorders

## Environmental Risk Factors

- Relational or social loss
- Easy access to lethal means
- Local clusters of suicide that have a contagious influence.

## Sociocultural Risk Factors

- Lack of social support and sense of isolation

- Stigma associated with help-seeking behavior
- Certain cultural and religious beliefs
- Influence of others who have died by suicide by exposure to the media or other sources.
- Barriers to assessing substance abuse health care treatment

Source: National Strategy for Suicide Prevention

Appendix B

# Glossary

**Adolescence** - the period of physical and psychological development from the onset of puberty to maturity.

**Biopsychosocial approach** - an approach to suicide prevention that focuses on those biological, psychological and social factors that may be causes, correlates, and/or consequences of mental health or mental illness and that may affect suicidal behavior.

**Causal factor** - a condition that alone is sufficient to produce a disorder.

**Community** - a group of people residing in the same locality or sharing a common interest.

**Comprehensive suicide prevention plans** - plans that use a multifaceted approach to addressing the problem; for example, including interventions targeting biopsychosocial, social and environmental factors.

**Connectedness** - closeness to an individual, group or people within a specific organization, perceived caring by others; satisfaction with relationship to others, or feeling loved and wanted by others.

**Contagion** - A phenomenon whereby susceptible persons are influenced towards suicidal behavior through knowledge of another person's suicidal acts.

**Depression** - a constellation of emotional, cognitive and somatic signs and symptoms, including sustained sad mood or lack of pleasure.

**Effective** - prevention programs that have been scientifically evaluated and shown to decrease an adverse outcome or increase a beneficial one in the target group more than in a comparison group.

**Environmental approach** - an approach that attempts to influence either the physical environment (such as reducing access to lethal means) or the social environment (such as providing work or academic opportunities).

**Frequency** - the number of occurrences of a disease or injury in a given unit of time; with respect to suicide, frequency applies only to suicidal behaviors which can repeat over time.

**Gatekeepers** - those individuals in a community who have face-to-face contact with large numbers of community members as part of their usual routine; they may be trained to identify persons at risk of suicide and refer them to treatment or supporting services as appropriate.

**Health** - the complete state of physical, mental, and social well-being, not merely the absence of disease or infirmity.

**Methods** - actions or techniques which result in an

individual inflicting self-harm (i.e., asphyxiation, overdose, jumping).

**Mental health** - the capacity of individuals to interact with one another and the environment in ways that promote subjective well-being, optimal development and use of mental abilities (cognitive, affective and relational).

**Mental health problem** - diminished cognitive, social or emotional abilities but not to the extent that the criteria for a mental disorder are met.

**Outcome** - a measurable change in the health of an individual or group of people that is attributable to an intervention.

**Prevention** - a strategy or approach that reduces the likelihood of risk of onset, or delays the onset of adverse health problems or reduces the harm resulting from conditions or behaviors.

**Protective factors** - factors that make it less likely that individuals will develop a disorder; protective factors may encompass biological, psychological or social factors in the individual, family and environment.

**Psychache** - severe, intolerable mental pain, causing suicide.

**Psychiatry** - the medical science that deals with the origin, diagnosis, prevention, and treatment of mental disorders.

**Psychology** - the science concerned with the individual behavior of humans, including mental and physiological processes related to behavior.

**Rate** - the number per unit of the population with a particular characteristic, for a given unit of time.

**Risk factors** - those factors that make it more likely that individuals will develop a disorder; risk factors may encompass biological, psychological or social factors in the individual, family and environment.

**Self-harm** - the various methods by which individuals injure themselves, such as self-laceration, self-battering, taking overdoses or exhibiting deliberate recklessness.

**Sociocultural approach** - an approach to suicide prevention that attempts to affect the society at large, or particular subcultures within it, to reduce the likelihood of suicide (such as adult-youth mentoring programs designed to improve the well-being of youth.

**Social services** - organized efforts to advance human welfare, such as home-delivered meal programs, support groups, and community recreation projects.

**Social support** - assistance that may include companionship, emotional backing, cognitive guidance, material aid and special services.

**Specialty treatment centers (e.g., mental health/substance abuse)** - health facilities where the personnel and resources focus on specific aspects of psychological or behavioral well-being.

**Stigma** - an object, idea, or label associated with disgrace or reproach.

**Substance abuse** - a maladaptive pattern of substance use manifested by recurrent and significant adverse consequences related to repeated use; includes maladaptive use of legal substances such as alcohol; prescription drugs such as analgesics, sedatives, tranquilizers, and stimulants; and illicit drugs such as marijuana, cocaine, inhalants, hallucinogens and heroin.

**Suicidal act (also referred to as suicide attempt)** - a potentially self-injurious behavior for which there is evidence that the person probably intended to kill himself or herself; a suicidal act may result in death, injuries, or no injuries.

**Suicidal behavior** - a spectrum of activities related to thoughts and behaviors that include suicidal thinking, suicide attempts, and completed suicide.

**Suicidal ideation** - self-reported thoughts of engaging in suicide-related behavior.

**Suicidality** - a term that encompasses suicidal thoughts, ideation, plans, suicide attempts, and completed suicide.

**Suicide** - death from injury, poisoning, or suffocation where there is evidence that a self-inflicted act led to the person's death.

**Suicide attempt** - a potentially self injurious behavior with a nonfatal outcome, for which there is evidence that the person intended to kill himself or herself; a suicide attempt may or may not result in injuries.

**Suicide attempt survivors** - individuals who have survived a prior suicide attempt.

**Suicide survivors** - family members, significant others, or acquaintances who have experienced the loss of a loved one due to suicide; sometimes this term is also used to mean suicide attempt survivors.

**Universal prevention intervention** - intervention targeted to a defined population, regardless of risk; (this could be an entire school, for example, and not the general population per se).

Source: National Strategy for Suicide Prevention

## Appendix C

---

**F**ollowing a list of terms and a discussion of cultural and social phenomena, each major cultural group is examined more closely in Chapter 11.

## Terms Defined:

"Race" applies to a group of human beings who share a genetic heritage based on physical characteristics such as the color of skin and hair and shape of the eyes, nose, and lips distinctive enough to be identified as a separate human type.

"Culture" refers to learned behaviors, values, and beliefs, as well as patterns of living and interpersonal relationships that are shared and transmitted in a society by a particular group.

"Ethnocentrism" refers to the belief that one's own group is superior to others.

"Enculturation" is the process by which one assumes the behaviors, values, and beliefs of a given culture, adapting to it and taking on that particular cultural identity.

"Cultural deprivation" means that individuals are lacking in intelligence and achievement because they have failed to adopt values and styles of the majority culture. This term states an assumption rather than reflecting a fact.

"Culturally different" is a new expression used to refer

to a group whose culture differs from that of the dominant group.

"Cultural competence" refers to the astute knowledge and ability required to recognize and appreciate cultural differences.

"Ethnicity" refers to an affiliation to a group that shares a unique cultural, social, and linguistic identity. The group has in common distinctive identifying characteristics originating from a national or racial identity.

"Assimilation" occurs when an individual has a primary identification with the mainstream culture and little or none with his or her own ethnic culture.

"Anomie" is used by French sociologist Emile Durkheim, who pioneered the study of suicide, to describe a condition in which an individual is not given enough guidance and so feels emotionally alienated from his or her world. According to Durkheim, anomie can lead to suicide.

"Alienation" is a feeling that one is no longer part of one's group: a feeling of social isolation.

"Acculturation" is a process during which two autonomous cultures interact for a period of time. Extensive changes in cultural patterns, beliefs, values, and behaviors will occur in one or both cultures.

"Biculturalism" is the incorporation of two differing cultural forces, values, customs, or beliefs that allows an individual to function within two cultures.

"Language" is the most powerful transmitter of culture.

"Marginality" (marginal ethnic identity) is the situation in which an individual engages in frequent and sustained primary contacts across ethnic group lines, particularly racial, cultural, or religious lines, but is not fully a member of either group. Low ethnic identity can be particularly detrimental to the self-esteem of the marginal or isolated individual.

"Generations" in the United States: "First generation" refers to residents who are foreign-born. "Second generation" refers to offspring born in the United States to foreign-born parents. "Third generation refers to offspring who were born in the United States, with one or more foreign-born grandparents.

.

Appendix D

# Recommended Resources

## Support Groups and Organizations:

**American Academy of Child & Adolescent Psychiatry**

3615 Wisconsin Ave., NW
Washington, DC 20016-3007
Phone: 202/966-7300
Fax: 202/966-2891
Web site: www.aacap.org

**American Association of Suicidology**

4201 Connecticut Ave., NW
Suite 408
Washington, DC 20008
Phone: 202/237-2280
Fax: 202/237-2282
Web site: www.suicidology.org

**Amercian Foundation for Suicide Prevention**

120 Wall St., 22nd Floor

New York, NY 10005
Phone: 888/333-AFSP (toll free) 212/363-3500
Fax: 212/363-6237
Web site: www.afsp.org

## SA / VE (Suicide Awareness / Voices of Education)

P.O. Box 24507
Minneapolis, MN 55424-0507
Phone: 612/946-7998
Web site: www.save.org

## SPAN (Suicide Prevention Advocacy Network)

5034 Odin's Way
Marietta, GA 30068
Phone: 888/649-1366 (toll free)
Fax: 770/642-1419
Web site: www.spanusa.org

## Yellow Ribbon Suicide Prevention Program

P.O. Box 644
Westminster, CO 80030-0644
Phone: 303/429-3530
Fax: 303/426-4496
Web site: www.yellowribbon.org

## Screening for Mental Health, Inc.

Phone: 781/239-0071
Web site: www.mentalhealthscreening.org
Web site: www.stopasuicide.org

# Index

_____, "About Teen Suicide: Kids Health for Parents", Nemours Foundation, 2005 June, p. 2.

Abraham, S. H., *Sociology*, London: The English Universities Press Limited, 1966.

Amanth, J., *Adolescent Suicide: Contemporary Tragedy, Interface: Psychiatry and Medicine,* Del Almo Hospital, Summer, 1984.

Anthony, M. *Teenage Suicide: Spreading a Network of Caring Over Field of Athletic Competition,* Interscholastic Athletic Administration, Winter, 1987, Vol. 14, No. 2.

Banks, S., "Who's There for Families of Suicide?" Southern California Living Section, *Los Angeles Times*, March 7, 1999.

Banks, Sandy, "Sasha is Dead, but Why?" *Los Angeles Times*, Nov. 18, 2005, p.1, 30-31.

Beck, A., *Depression: Causes and Treatment*, Philadelphia, University of Pennsylvania Press,1985.

Benedek, Elissa P. and Catherine F. Brown, *How to Help Your Child Overcome Your Divorce,* American Psychiatric Press, Inc., Washington, DC. 1995

Bennet, W. J., *What Works: Schools Without Drugs*, U.S. Department of Education, 1986.

Bensing, Kay, "Unanswered Questions", *Advance for Nurses*, Oct. 31, 2005, p. 36.

_____, "Bergenfield's Tragic Foursome", *U.S. News and World Report*, March 23, 1987.

Berman, A. and D. Jobes, *Youth Suicide, A guide for Parents*, National Center for the Study and Prevention of Suicide, Washington, DC, 1991.

Betelheim, B., "Love & Death", By Celeste Fremon, *Los Angeles Times Magazine*, January 27, 1991

Blankenhorn, David, *Fatherless America*, New York, Harper Perennial, 1995

Blau, M., "After Divorce", *New Woman*, May, 1992, pp. 79-82.

Blau, M. *Families Apart*, New York, Putnam's Sons, 1993.

Brandis, C., L. Wolf et al., "The Association Between Immigrant Status and Risk—Behavior Patterns in Latin Adolescents", *Journal of Adolescent Health* 17 (.2), pp. 99-105, 1995.

Buchanan, C. M., E. E. Maccoby and S. M. Dornbush, *Adolescents After Divorce*, Cambridge, Harvard University Press, 1996.

Butterfield, F., "Culture of Suicide by Gun Haunts Rural USA", *New York Times*, 2005, Feb. 22, 4 pp.

Canneto, S. S. and I. Sakinofsky, "The Gender Paradox in Suicide", *Suicide and Life- Threatening Behavior*, Vol. 28 (*i*) Spring 1998.

Cannon, A. and C. Kleiner, "Teens Get Real", *US News and World Report*, April 17, 2000.

Celotta, B., "Preventing Teenage Suicide," *Education USA*, Washington DC, , 1986, Dec. 8, Vol. 29, No. 15.

Clinton, Hillary R., *It Takes A Village*, New York, Simon and Schuster, 1996.

Davidson, L. and M. Linnoila, *Social Isolation in Risk Factors for Youth Suicide*, New York, Hemisphere Publishing Corp., 1991.

Dobson, J., *Focus on the Family*, Weaton, Tyndale, 1985.

Durkheim, E., *Suicide: A Study in Sociology*, trans. J. A. Spaulding and G. Simpson, New York, Free Press, 1951.

Farberow, N. L., *Preparatory and Prior Suicidal Behavior Factors in Risk Factors for Youth Suicide*, edit. Lucy Davidson and Mark Linnoila, New York, Hemisphere Publishing Corp., 1991.

Francis, D. B., *Suicide: A Preventable Tragedy*, New York, Lodestar Books, E. P. Dutton, 1989.

Frankel, Bernard and Rachel Kranz, *Straight Talk About Teenage Suicide*, New York,

Facts on File, 1994.

Gardner, R., *The Parents' Book About Divorce*, New York, Doubleday & Co., 1977.

Gardner, Sandra and Gary Rosenberg, *Teenage Suicide*, (Revised Ed.), Englewood Cliffs, Julian Messner, 1990.

Giger, J. N. and R. E. Davidhizan, *Transcultural Nursing: Assessment and Intervention*, (Second Ed.), St. Louis, Mosley, 1995.

208

Harris, L., Hostile Hallways: *The AAUW Survey on Sexual Harassment in America's Schools*, Washington, DC, American Association of University Women Educational Foundation, 1993.

Hendin, H., *Suicide In America*, New York, W.W. Norton, 1983.

_____, Hispanic Youth Health Assessment Report, Multicultural Area Health Education

Los Angeles County, Washington, DC, CSSMHO Press, 1998.

Hoff Oberlin, L. *Surviving Separation and Divorce*, Holbrook, Adams Media Corp. 2000.

_____, "How to Talk to Your Kids About Drugs", Office of National Drug Control Policy,

*Los Angeles Times*, September 8, 1995.

Hurtado, Juan, *Counseling and Culture*, School of Education, San Diego State University, 1979.

Hyde, Margaret O. and Margaret H. Forsyth, Suicide, *The Hidden Epidemic*, Minneapolis,

Compcore Publishers, 181, 1986.

Katz, R., "Talk About Teens", *Children*, Winter 1995-1996.

Keefe, S., A. M. Padilla and M. L. Carlos, *Emotional Support Systems in Two Cultures: A Comparison of Mexican Americans and Angle Americans*, Spanish Speaking Mental Health Research Center, UCLA, 1975.

Kirk, W. G., *Adolescent Suicide: A School-Based Approach to Assessment and Intervention*, Champaign, Research Press, 1993.

Kubler-Ross, E., *Living With Death and Dying*, New York, MacMillan, 1982.

Lafromboise, T.D., D. S. Bigfoot, "Culture and Cognitive Considerations in the Prevention of American Indian Adolescent Suicide", *Journal of Adolescence*, 11, 139-153, 1988.

Leder, Jane Mersky, *Dead Serious*, New York, Athenum, 1987.

Leshner, A. I., *Preventing Drug Use Among Children and Adolescents A research-Based Guide*, National Institute of Health, 1997.

Lightner, C., *Giving Sorrow Words*, New York, Warren Books, 1990.

Litman, R. E. and N. L. Faberow, "Pop-rock Music As a Precipitating Cause in Youth Suicide", *Journal of Forensic Sciences*, 29, 494-499.

Louks, J. and G. Otis, *Effects of Divorce on Teenage Suicide*, Research Paper & Presentation: American Association of Suicidiology, 2000.

Males, M. A., *The Scapegoat Generation: America's War on Adolescents*, Monroe, Common Courage Press, 2001.

Marquardt, Elizabeth, "The Children Left Behind," *Los Angeles Times*, Opinion Section, November 11, 2005, p. B11.

Mednick, F., *Rebel Without a Car: Surviving and Appreciation Your Child's Teenage Years*, In Kirk, W.G. Adolescent Suicide: A School-Based Approach, Champaign, Research Press, 1993.

_____, *Myth of the (Black) Teen Suicide Epidemic, The*, Alter-Net., 2001, 3, July 2001

Oliver, Myrna, Dr. Joseph D. Teicher, Psychiatrist, Director of Child Guidance Clinic, *Los Angeles Times*, August 28, 2000.

Padilla, Amando, *Hispanic Psychology—Critical Issues in Theory and Research*, Thousand Oaks, Sage Publications, 1995.

Peck, M., "Suicide Prevention", *Los Angeles Times*, August 19, 1993.

Poussaint, A. and H. Alexander, *Lay My Burden Down*, Boston, Beacon Press, 2000.

Powell, K. *Compassionate Friends: A Newsletter*, Ormond Beach, FL, November, 1999.

Rader, Dotson, "I Was Ready for Anything", *Los Angeles Times Parade Magazine*, 4-5, Sunday, July 30, 2000,

Reams, B., *Personal Communications*, Los Angeles, 2001.

Rimm, S., *On Raising Kids*, Watertown, Educational Assessment Services, 2000.

Robinson, R., *Survivors of Suicide*, Santa Monica, IBS Press, 1989.

Rogers, F. and B. Head, *Mister Rogers Talks With Parents*, Pittsburg, Family Communications, 1983.

Rosenberg, G. and S. Gardner, *Teenage Suicide*, Boston, Julian Messner, 1990.

Rosenberg, M., *Suicide Clusters*, Centers for Disease Control and Prevention, Suicide Among Children, Adolescents and Young Adults, 1980-1992, MMWR 1995, 44:289.

Rosenbert, E., *Get A Clue*, New York, Henry Holt, 1999.

Rosof, B. N., *The Worst Loss*, New York, Henry Holt & Co., 1994.

Ross, C., "Youth Suicide Epidemic Confronting Nation's Schools", *School Board News*, August 14, 1985.

Rubin, R., *Adolescent Suicide Prevention in Schools*, American Suicidiology Conference, Los Angeles, 2000.

Satir, V., *Conjoint Family Therapy*, Palo Alto, Science and Behavior Books, 1983.

Shneidman, E., Suicide as Psychache: *A Clinical Approach To Self-Destructive Behavior*, Northvale, NJ, Jason Aronson, 34-57, 1993.

Shneidman, E., "Suicide Prevention", *The Los Angeles Times*, Aug. 19, 1993.

Shneidman, E., "Suicide as psychache: a commentary, *A Journal of Nervous and Mental Disease*", 181(3), 145-147, 1993.

Shneidman, E., *The Definition of Suicide*, Wiley & Sons, New York, 119-149, 1985.

Shneidman, E., "A multi-psychological approach to suicide and suicide prevention", Youth Suicide Conference, UCLA, April 23, 1988.

Shneidman, E., Mandelkorn, "Suicide—It Doesn't Have to Happen", *Some Facts About*

*Suicide*, PHS Publication, Vol. 852, U.S. Government Printing Office, 1966. Schoen, C., K. Davis, K. S. Collins, L. Greenberg, C. Des Roches, and M. Abrams, *The Commonwealth Fund survey of Health of Adolescent Girls*, New York, Commonwealth Fund, 1997.

212

Schuster, C. S. and S. S. Asburn, The Process of Human Development, Boston, Little Brown & Co., 1986.

_____, "Some Things You Should Know About Preventing Teen Suicide", American Academy of Pediatrics, 2, 2005.

Simmons, Ann M., "In Search of Juvenile Justice", *Los Angeles Times*, Oct. 26, 2005, p.1.

Steinberg, L. B., B. Brown, and F. Dornbusch, *Beyond The Classroom*, New York, Simon and Schuster, 1997.

Stonequist, F. U., *The Marginal Man: A Study of Personality and Culture Conflict*, New York, Russel & Russel, Inc., 1937.

_____, Suicide and Attempted Suicide," *Morbidity and Mortality Weekly Report*, Vol., 53, No. 22, 2005 Feb.

_____, "Suicide Fact Sheet", *CDC*, 2004, Dec. 22.

_____, *Teen Suicide*, American Academy of Child and Adolescent Psychiatry, No. 10, 5, 2004

_____, *Teen Suicide*, NAMI, Nation's voice on Mental Illness, 5, 2005.

_____, *Teen Suicide: An Act of Desperation or Escapism?* India Nest, 3, 2005

_____, *Teenage Suicide: Education and Prevention*, Coleman Professional Services, 2, 2002.

_____, "Youth Risk Behavior Surveillance, *CDC*, United States", MMWR, 1998, 47, 1997.

Woods, D., "Risk factors associated with suicidal ideation in substance abusing adolescent and young adult males." Unpublished dissertation, The Claremont Graduate School, 1990.

Woods, D. S., "The hospitalized adolescent", Continuing education seminar presented at Kaiser Mental Health Center, Los Angeles, Nov. 3, 1992.

Woods, D. S. & P. H. Dreyer, "Suicidal ideation and ego identity status in late adolescent male substance abusers and non-abusers", Poster session presented at the Conference on Adolescence, Educational Testing Service, Atlanta, 1990.

Yoshino, Kim et al, "Killer Sought Solace Online", *Los Angeles Times*, Nov. 1, 2005, p.1, 12.

# About The Author

Dorris S. Woods, Ph.D., RN, CS, is a community mental health specialist. As a former associate professor, she lectured on psychiatric/mental in the Department of Health and Human Services, California State University at Long Beach.

Dr. Woods has conducted workshops on in-patient adolescent therapy, studies into suicide, and has written numerous articles on child abuse, child safety and adolescent suicide.

Her publications include: "A Sharp Rise in Black Teenage Suicide," Los Angeles Sentinel and The United Methodist Review, Bellringer, 2004; "Understanding Adolescent Suicide: A desperate Response to Psychache," Nurse Week, 1996; "Vulnerability as a Factor in Adolescent Suicide," Los Angeles Sentinel, 1996; Failure to Cope: A handbook for suicide Prevention, 1991.

Dr. Woods resides in Culver City, California with her dog, "Cookie." She welcomes comments and feedback from readers. You may contact her at P. O. Box 3093, Culver City, CA 90230.

ISBN 1412085565-9

Made in the USA